I0438568

Bouncing Back
From Loss

HOW TO LEARN
FROM YOUR PAST,
HEAL THE PRESENT,
AND TRANSFORM
YOUR FUTURE

Donna Marie Thompson, Ph.D

NEW YORK

Bouncing Back From Loss

How to Learn from Your Past, Heal the Present, and Transform Your Future

by DONNA MARIE THOMPSON, PhD

ISBN 978-1-60037-825-6 (paperback)

Library of Congress Control Number: 2010936650

Published by:

MORGAN JAMES PUBLISHING
The Entrepreneurial Publisher
5 Penn Plaza, 23rd Floor
New York City, New York 10001
(212) 655-5470 Office
(516) 908-4496 Fax
www.MorganJamesPublishing.com

Cover Design by:
3 Dog Design
www.3dogdesign.net

Interior Design by:
Bonnie Bushman
bbushman@bresnan.net

In an effort to support local communities, raise awareness and funds, Morgan James Publishing donates one percent of all book sales for the life of each book to Habitat for Humanity.
Get involved today, visit
www.HelpHabitatForHumanity.org.

I dedicate this book to my Teacher,
the glorious and merciful God,

and to his faithful servant,
Mary Mueller, my mother,
a warm and courageous spirit,

and to mothers everywhere for all they do.

"*Donna Marie has put together a very powerful resource not only for those who have reached the end of their rope, but also a wonderful tool that can be respectfully given to those suffering from loss to help them cope and recover. Donna Marie's inspiring story contains specific strategies that anyone can recreate to get back on top of the world.*"

David Riklan, Founder of SelfGrowth.com and bestselling author

"*Life can be challenging and Donna Marie was hit hard physically, emotionally, and financially. For those who have experienced loss, her journey from despair to victory can be helpful to you.*"

Margaret Paul, PhD, Inner Bonding, Healing Your Aloneness and Author of *Do I Have To Give Up Me To Be Loved By You?*

"Bouncing Back From Loss *will truly help you bounce back. Healing is a process. The light at the end of that process is your own peace of mind, joy, and happiness. Are you ready?*"

Aurora Winter, Author of *From Heartbreak to Happiness*, Founder of The Grief Coach Academy

"*What a story! What a recovery! What guts! I deal with this sort of thing a lot in my practice and I can completely relate to what Donna Marie is saying. So much so that I recommend* Bouncing Back From Loss *to my clients. Donna Marie's personal story is heartbreaking but she refuses to stay down, she gets right back up. Donna Marie refuses to see herself as a victim, she is a victor. It is positively encouraging and inspiring.*"

Gary Powell, Success Coach and Master NLP Practitioner

"We all know that perseverance can overcome the challenges we encounter. We're quick to offer this advice…but still, we all end up in tough situations. Donna Marie overcame many early obstacles yet went on to live a good life. Then the unthinkable happened. But she took it in stride. Donna Marie offers suggestions that will help you bounce back from whatever life has thrown at you. It's smart to avoid life's obstacles and even smarter to be prepared for a few you just can't avoid. You'll see for yourself when you read Bouncing Back From Loss. *An inspirational story and down-to-earth plan for prosperity, no matter what."*

Warren Whitlock, BestSellerAuthors.com

"Donna Marie's story is not only a compelling and fascinating read, it is also a lesson in perseverance, personal motivation and accomplishment in the face of extreme adversity. If you have ever fallen into the trap of feeling sorry for yourself because of adversities that you are facing, Bouncing Back From Loss *is a fabulous reality check for you. Even better, it will be a remarkable motivator. Donna Marie's story is truly one of the most motivational and inspiring I have ever read!"*

Rob Coats, Connectionaire, Award Winning Entrepreneur, and bestselling Author of *Connect and Grow Rich*

"Donna Marie shares with us her incredible story of loss, learning, and life's blessings. It is a valuable insight into the gift of being resilient and mastering the art of bouncing back. While many of us may struggle with losing a parent, the demise of a close relationship, challenges with our health, and a serious financial crisis, it is a rare individual who conquers all of these in the same short time frame and comes out on top. Donna Marie does so with fortitude, persistence and an unsinkable spirit. Her saga offers hope, encouragement, and solutions no matter where you are in your life."

Melissa Galt, Founder, Today by Design Institute, Author of *Celebrate Your Life*

"I loved Bouncing Back From Loss. *The emotional attachment you feel as you take a front-row seat through Donna Marie's struggles is amazing.* Bouncing Back From Loss *takes you on a complete journey from the depths of despair to*

the exhilaration of victory. The practical action steps, resources and real-life lessons to overcoming anything thrown your way are exceptional. Bouncing Back From Loss is a complete, genuine "map for life" I'd recommend to anyone struggling through life's ups and downs. Excellent!"

Joni Waseity Beadle, Author of *In Sickness and in Wealth*, Entrepreneur that changes lives spiritually, emotionally, physically, socially and financially, insicknessandinwealth.com

"An inspiring tale of a courageous journey through life, Donna Marie pours her triumph over the trials and tribulations of loss onto the pages of enlightenment and spiritual awakening. From cover to cover, Bouncing Back From Loss *provides a map for finding your way out of the shadows of physical, emotional, financial, and spiritual strife. A must-read."*

J. Todd Rhoad, Director, BT Consulting and Author of *Blitz the Ladder: A Team-based Approach to Getting Ahead in Business*

"After reading just the first ten pages, I was totally hooked. Bouncing Back From Loss *is so well written, intertwining the emotions of loss, betrayal, hope, and happiness that it reads like a novel. Even if you aren't in a loss situation,* Bouncing Back From Loss *is well worth reading and introducing to anyone who needs to find hope and happiness. Kudos to Donna Marie—a real survivor who is empowering others with her 5 Es to Recovery coaching program, a formula well worth following to get true results."*

Sharon Pierce McCullough, CCO of ZiggityZoom.com

"If you've suffered a devastating loss, Bouncing Back From Loss *is for you. Donna Marie uses her personal story to teach and inspire you to bounce back from challenges no matter what they are - financial, emotional, or physical. Using incredible insight and wisdom Donna Marie helps you unshackle the chains of loss to experience the freedom of living life fully each day and achieving your dreams."*

Greta Jaeger, LPC, PLCC, LMT, Founder of Coaching Your Dreams, CoachingYourDreams.com

"Nothing inspires and captures the hearts and minds of people more than the ability to bounce back from total devastation. It's the one trait that turns ordinary people into extraordinary heroes and catapults them to new frontiers they never thought possible. Donna Marie's story depicts the very essence of this trait and fully enshrines its pillars. Her priceless insights and valuable tools give you the precise road map you need to transform your life too. I wholeheartedly recommend Bouncing Back From Loss - *it's a timeless masterpiece."*

Erfan Hettini, Author of *101 Reasons You Should Fire Your Employer & Start Your Own Business*, fire-your-employer.com

"A compelling story with demonstrated inspiring results. Readers can immediately apply Donna Marie's insights to their lives and create powerful and sustainable change. Bouncing Back From Loss *is for you if you are in the process of bouncing back or would like to prepare for an empowered future."*

Bruce D Schneider, PhD, MCC. Founder of Institute for Professional Excellence in Coaching and bestselling Author of *Energy Leadership*

"Yes, you CAN make it! We all know this, but it's very encouraging to read someone else's story to confirm this within ourselves. And that's exactly what Bouncing Back From Loss *does for anyone who is struggling with loss or struggling to just survive. There is indeed a bright light at the end of the tunnel. And it is only five steps away. It is deeply heartening to note that what appear at first to be set-BACKs in your life are actually set-UPs for your new and positively energized future!"*

Mark Freeman, founder of EpicWealthStrategies.com

"Sometimes we experience loss at such a deep and profound level that we think we'll never be able to recover. Thank goodness for Donna Marie and her willingness to share her personal experiences with major losses and setbacks in many areas of life. Donna Marie shows you how she not only mastered recovery from grief and loss, but also went on to create a satisfying and thriving new life! If you find yourself coping with the aftershocks of a major setback in your life, then Bouncing Back From Loss *can help you. Donna Marie offers solutions, strategies, and most importantly, action steps*

you can implement immediately to start the healing process. It doesn't matter where you are in your journey to wholeness, Donna Marie's easy-to-follow 5Es to Recovery program will work. There is hope. Recovery is possible. And with Donna Marie, you won't have to do it alone".

Paula Tarrant, Spiritual Life Coach and
Transformation Expert, InspiredWomenWork.com

"Donna Marie has provided you with a true-life exposé of the events that led up to four major losses in her life—any one of which would have been devastating on its own. Having her life literally up-ended, Donna Marie has bounced back from devastation—and she has bounced back in style. The deeply personal dialogues give the reader a front row seat into the action and the swirling emotions. Amazingly, Donna Marie rose triumphant. In a unique feature of Bouncing Back From Loss, *she shares her lessons and very practical tools to help you develop a stronger, more balanced way of living.* Bouncing Back From Loss *is a must-read for all who have personally experienced loss in their life or those who know others who have."*

Dr. Douglas H. Fitzgerald, CEO and founder of Boomer-Living.com

*"*Bouncing Back From Loss *is a courageous story of loss, healing, and rebirth. Donna Marie's thoughtful reflection on her own journey through loss will no doubt serve as a source of strength and faith to others."*

Reverend Jenny Cannon

"Whether you are experiencing financial, physical, or emotional loss, in Bouncing Back From Loss *Donna Marie shows you the key steps to recovering from upheaval so that you thrive in the aftermath. By relating her personal experience and through the colorful dialogues, Donna Marie shows that even those of us who think we are prepared can be devastated by a series of events that are not within our control. With her innovative 5 Es to Recovery program, Donna Marie provides you with a step-by-step guide noting specific action steps to help you create your own personalized road map to recovery without feeling overwhelmed."*

Laurie Tossy, Author of *Refuse to Diet: Weight Loss Success Starts with Your Mind...Not Your Mouth,* RefuseToDiet.com

"The 5Es provide an essential road map for your own bouncing back journey. After you decide you're ready to start, the 5Es are just the ticket to guide you. They also help you to identify and remove obstacles that are blocking your path. The 5Es provides you with step-by-step actions to keep you moving forward at your own pace toward the more satisfying life of your dreams. Break free now!"

Laura Hall, Certified Professional Coach, Hall Coaching

"Donna Marie's courageous story of personal and professional empowerment, strength, and persistence will inspire and empower anyone attempting to deal with pressing life issues. As I read Bouncing Back From Loss, *I felt a personal connection to her and the events of her life. She is truly a survivor in every sense of the word and will deeply touch the lives of those* Bouncing Back From Loss; *this book will be a primary resource in my practice and in my life. Thank you Donna Marie for sharing your inspirational and insightful journey."*

Audrey Gemberling, M.A., Corporate Health Coach / Risk Management Consultant, Crossroads to Change, LLC, audreyg@crossroadstochange.com

"Donna Marie is a courageous woman who has triumphed over the tough challenges life threw at her. In the process she developed a wonderful set of insightful resources that can be used to make powerful changes to transform your life when facing emotional, physical, or financial loss. Thank you Donna Marie for sharing your inspiring story and creating the 5Es workbook to empower those in despair to find their inner strength and succeed with confidence."

Gitie House, WingedHearts.Org

"Donna Marie's positive, affirming, and thoughtful manner bolsters my confidence every time I seek her counsel. She consistently enables me to think more broadly and imaginatively about worries and situations."

Abigail B. Wiebenson, Certified Personal and Leadership Coach

"Donna Marie first shares her story of deep loss and disappointment. But more importantly, she then demonstrates how she recovered and how you can, too. Bouncing Back From Loss *is chock full of wonderful tools for full*

recovery from any loss. Learn from each experience and get stronger, just as she has. An inspirational guidebook."

Snowden McFall, bestselling Author of *Fired Up!*
How to Succeed by Making Your Dreams Come True.
President, Brightwork Advertising & Training, Inc.

"Donna Marie shows that we go through life with its ups and downs and proves we can rebound. Bouncing Back From Loss is proof that no one goes through life untested. No pressure no diamonds."

Ken Bossone, Author of *Why Positive Thinkers Have the Power*,
President of World Positive Thinkers Club

"You can follow the same five steps that Donna Marie took to bounce back from loss yourself. Donna Marie's proven tools will not only help you but they also offer a road map for you to reach out and help others. This inspirational story gives hope to those struggling with life's unexpected challenges. Everyone that reads Bouncing Back From Loss *will take away something that will help them to improve their life."*

Pat Bluth, author *From Pain to Peace—*
A Journey from Rage to Forgiveness, patbluth.com

"I couldn't put Bouncing Back From Loss *down! A powerful saga outlining massive challenges that occurred in a fairly short period of time, Donna Marie frankly shows us the path into the problems, the lessons learned, and offers a clear path to recovery. If you've ever had to deal with the issues of an aging parent, a troubled relationship, or a physical setback that alters your existence,* Bouncing Back From Loss *will help you get back on track."*

Faye Levow, President & CEO, Launch Pad Publishing, Inc.,
Author of *OMG! My Parents are Getting OLD!*

Table of Contents

FOREWORD TO

Bouncing Back From Loss

By Judith Parker Harris

Both individuals and our society at large have now been through a tough few years, and **Bouncing Back From Loss** arrives just in time to show us three critical skills - how to cope, survive, and thrive. These skills are powerfully conveyed with valuable experience and warm encouragement by Donna Marie Thompson.

Life seems to come at us in threes. In Hollywood, there's a saying that celebrity deaths come in threes. In comedy, there's the "Rule of 3"; in music there's the rhythm of three in the waltz. As I read **Bouncing Back From Loss**, I was struck by the feeling that perhaps our major life transformations are guided by three powerful emotions hitting us simultaneously. For Donna Marie, it was fear, loss, and betrayal – all at the same time. She tells a captivating story weaving these emotions together as intricately as a Viennese waltz and with as much dramatic tension as a BlockBuster movie.

As Donna Marie falls backward from the punch of her mother's death, her fiancé's betrayal, her own near financial ruin, plus a serious physical injury, she is not knocked out. No, that will not do. Instead, she rallies with the force of her own triple threat – Beliefs, Personal Growth, and Reaching Out to Help Others. Donna Marie picks up the pieces of her life and emerges as a knowing guide, coach, and teacher. Her plan is so simple that it is, quite honestly, brilliant.

Here's the empowering truth she shares: When you are suffering, you are yearning for effective, proven ways to get back on your feet and regain your strength. Your experience is like no one else's. You are looking for a path that will work for you – a way out of your pain. If you're reading this now, you are suffering in some way; from a broken relationship or emotional loss, an injury or illness, a financial loss, or some other setback. Isn't it comforting to know that the 5Es to Recovery program can work for you? As you experience each **E** in Donna Marie's innovative approach, you will have the healing actions laid out for you in manageable steps that will advance your own personal recovery journey.

As we emerge from a crisis, any crisis, we often feel victimized. Donna Marie shows us how to shed those feelings and re-connect with our inner power – the power to heal; the power that we all possess. As you experience Donna Marie's 5**E**s to Recovery, when you are ready you will choose three emotions to **E**xplore. You will **E**liminate your unwanted feelings in the second **E**. Then, step-by-step, you are guided to **E**mbrace your situation, **E**nvision a new future, and **E**nergize your world to round out the 5Es. Somewhere along the way you will discover that what you thought of as your "current comfort zone" is actually exceedingly uncomfortable and that the cost of staying stuck there is way too high.

I am a movie producer, author, and speaker; for the past 20 years I have coached hundreds of people to bust through their blocks. I am pleased to report that I had an epiphany while reading **Bouncing Back From Loss**. My epiphany dealt with why I hesitate to tell my "Recovery from Multiple Sclerosis" story to all of my audiences. When following the 5Es, I realized that I had not forgiven myself for my own role in my loss. Yes, I had my own big three events – MS diagnosis, fiancé disappeared, and business loss. Now I've forgiven myself, and I join with Donna Marie in encouraging all of you to honor and share your stories of recovery.

Whatever your situation, whatever your loss, begin with the gift of recovery that **Bouncing Back From Loss** will give you. Then be fortified by its empowering guidance. And finally, be amazed by the story that *you* will weave; your new and brighter future awaits. As Donna Marie advises, "Where you finish will not be limited by where you start."

Judith Parker Harris
Producer
Author **Conquer Crisis with Health-Esteem**
Blocked to BlockBuster Coach
www.BlockedtoBlockBuster.com

Introduction

In the span of a few months, I lost everything I held dear. Perhaps you've gone through a similar situation and feel hopeless. If you are suffering from an emotional or financial loss, there is hope and there is help. I lost my mother, my man, my money, and my health—within a short period of time. Yet, with determination, I conquered devastation and multiple concurrent setbacks. I endured. I survived. I bounced back, and you can too.

The Far-reaching Effects of Loss

When we suffer a significant loss in our lives, it results in a major setback with multiple domino effects that linger well beyond the immediate event. For example, a relationship break-up can extend well beyond the loss of a soul mate and end up causing us to doubt our own self-worth and basic lovability.

Amid financial loss, there is the loss of money and disappointment that some of our dreams will not be fulfilled as planned, but the aftermath may involve a deep jolt to our egos that calls into question our basic ability to make our own way in the world. Our financial worth is often inextricably linked to our self-worth, which can go up or down depending upon external circumstances.

> *Our financial worth is often inextricably linked to our self-worth, which can go up or down depending upon external circumstances.*

With the loss of a parent—either physically or emotionally—feelings of inadequacy and powerlessness along with self-doubts can be devastating and long lasting. I have not experienced the loss of a spouse or a child—the feelings that envelop you must be unimaginable. My mother lived a full life to 81 years, and I am thankful for that —yet even having said that, I was still reeling from the loss and the events that led up to it for almost two years.

In addition to the actual event itself and the resulting loss, the add-on effects can intensify our feelings of loss. Each hopeless moment undermines our confidence, weakens our judgment, drags us down, and builds on our previous repository of self-doubts. When this goes on too long, the effects are pure poison to our bodies and our lives.

...we all possess a strength buried within us to overcome the loss, build back our lives...

Despite the ill effects of loss, we all possess a strength buried within us to overcome the loss, build back our lives, and eventually move forward again. My aim is to help you find your own path to recovery so that you, too, may once again feel whole.

Preface

I hit bottom. I was knocked for a loop. I was devastated, but somehow, some way, I pulled my life together and got back on my feet. I assessed my values, re-evaluated my priorities, examined what I wanted, and drove myself forward. Now, I'm living a marvelous life. Yes, I'm back, better than ever and feeling great. Today, there's a spring in my step, a smile on my face, and things are looking bright. I have a new direction, and I live out my purpose every day.

It wasn't always so promising. For several excruciating months, I felt the weight of the world on my shoulders. I thought my life was ending. Perhaps you've been (or are) there in the pit of despair. Take heart, because I have a message that will change your outlook, your life, and your purpose.

As a successful businesswoman, I built on my strong points, experience, and business knowledge to make my way back. I took inventory, assessed myself and my possibilities, and found what I needed to carry on. In the process, I learned many lessons that I am prepared to share with you now.

In the upcoming chapters, I'll explain how you can avoid some of the same mistakes in your life. I'll point out the warning signs and the steps to take toward emotional recovery. Moreover, if you're already stuck in an awful trap, I'll show you key steps to increase your leverage and improve your situation.

Most of all, this book will stir your mind and your passion. It will generate feelings and help you develop inspiring solutions that will work for you. It will help you stand tall, not be a victim, and get what you truly want out of life.

...this book will stir your mind and your passion.

Structure of the Book

This book is divided into sixteen chapters. I encourage you to read them all from beginning to end to gain the full context and absorb all of the messages. But if you are much more interested in some particular topics, this book is conveniently structured so that you can first focus on the sections and topics that are of most interest to you and then go back to the other sections later.

This is my story of triumph over trials and tribulations—conquering devastation with determination. My story details four different bouncing-back-from-loss segments as follows:

- Elder care setback
- Health setback
- Emotional relationship setback
- Financial setback

The first five chapters set the tone for the story. They describe the forces swirling around me over the course of this saga. Chapters 6 through 10 describe the emotional, physical, and financial setbacks. Chapters 11 through 13 focus on my recovery in multiple dimensions and the lessons that I learned in the process. Hopefully, through these lessons, perhaps you can avoid some of the mistakes that I have made.

The final three chapters (Chapters 14-16) outline a powerful recovery process, the 5 Es to Recovery (Explore, Eliminate, Embrace, Envision, and Energize) that are designed to help others bounce back from loss, and also feature a chapter on 7 Obstacles to Recovery.

The appendices feature a timeline to track the multiple threads of the story, quizzes to assess your current status, details on the 5 Es to Recovery Program, keys to business start-ups, and a suggested reading list.

Author's Note

To know how far I've come, you must know where I've been. After months in and out of the ICU and long-term care facilities with hopeful periods of recovery and moments of utter despair, my eighty-one-year-old mother—my friend, companion, and champion against my father's gender prejudice—lost her battle with health concerns caused by a medical error. While my mother was still in the ICU on a ventilator, my decades-long relationship with my then fiancé began deteriorating. Growing controlling and even threatening, John became an unwanted tenant, hijacking control of my house and consequently blocking my retirement.

Two months after my mother's death, as we struggled over the decision to sell my home, I suffered from a pinched a nerve in my neck, a debilitating injury that left me in constant pain and only able to work half days. Because I delayed selling my house due to John's threats, protests, and blockades, I lost a huge amount of money that I had earmarked for retirement due to the drop in home prices (the initial sale of the home would have been for $725,000, but instead, it sold for $370,000), and I was forced to delay my long-planned retirement and continue working.

After three long years of conflict, the foundation of our relationship had cracked beyond repair (which began seven months before the death of my mother); like a slow-acting poison, our relationship sadly

After three long years of conflict, the foundation of our relationship had cracked beyond repair

and devastatingly grew toxic and unhealthy due to his threats, betrayals, controlling behavior, and empty promises. Eventually, I was forced to sever all ties with the man I had believed to be my one true soul mate for the past twenty years.

That is where I have been.

But today, I am happy. I approach life with joy. I am equipped to handle what life throws at me. I am ready, I am able, I am confident, and I am stable. I take responsibility for my actions. I am resilient. I am a survivor. I am empowered to tackle the tough things. When I fall, as I inevitably will, I will pick myself up. I have faith, and I have courage.

> *I am ready, I am able, I am confident, and I am stable.*

Sadly, it wasn't always so. Happily, it is now.

Today, I am a healthy, successful, fulfilled woman on my way to financial independence, again. I am surrounded by friends. I am connected to many people. I make new connections all the time—with ease. I am working full time, and I am an entrepreneur on the side. I am a victor, not a victim. I have healed, specifically by using the 5 Es to Recovery (Explore, Eliminate, Embrace, Envision, and Energize). My best days are indeed ahead of me and yours can be too.

CHAPTER I

Today All Is Well

"Hope is the dream of a soul awake."
– French proverb

1. My Physical Profile Today

*"Take care of your body with steadfast fidelity. The soul must see through
these eyes alone, and if they are dim, the whole world is clouded."*
– Goethe

Today, I am healthier than I have been in a long, long time. Even as I
am getting older, I am in good shape. I know and accept the proper course
for my physical health. I make an effort to take care of myself—but not
obsessively. Now I can sleep through the night. Ah, the magnificent healing
power of sleep!

I have lost more than thirty pounds of excess weight. I've conquered
some of the demons of emotional eating and tamed the inner voice that tried
to relieve my pain with food—mostly sugar. Now, I am aware of my eating
options and keep my body on an even keel. I experiment with fruits and
vegetables and new ways to prepare them and make them fun. The plan
worked reasonably well, but then my weight plateaued. Oh no, the middle-
aged woman stuck with the muffin top. No, I demand to have a waist! I
started on Nutrisystem for the final twenty pounds and when you see me,

you'll notice the results. I can barely contain my euphoria when the waistband on my skirt is loose—oh, what a feeling!

Fitness

Last year, amazingly, I skated in an in-line half-marathon. They closed the streets for us; it was incredible to skate on the roads without worrying about the cars. Most importantly, I finished the race; and I did not finish last in my first timed event. Interestingly enough, the skaters behind me were all younger. It is funny though. Among skaters, I'm a wimp; among non-skaters, I'm Wonder Woman!

Now, when time and weather permit, I skate nine miles a day after work in a park by the river. As for skating conditions, it must be dry and the temperature at least 40 degrees including the wind chill factor—any lower than that is downright painful. I also play tennis. I kayak. I dance. I hike. I have been known to swing a golf club or two. Today, I am healthy, agile, and fit.

2. My Financial Profile Today

"I believe the power to make money is a gift from God... to be developed and used to the best of our ability for the good of mankind."
— John D. Rockefeller

Today, I am saving for my retirement. I have all of the letters: IRA, IRA rollover, Roth 401k, and even a small pension. I invest conservatively based on two newsletter advisers that I follow.

I evaluate all my major purchases and consider their impact on my retirement lifestyle—not my current lifestyle.

I evaluate all my major purchases and consider their impact on my retirement lifestyle—not my current lifestyle. I know that as I prepare to retire, every dollar that I save goes toward rebuilding my capital base. The magic of capital is that your money makes money—true passive income. Even though interest rates might be low at times, they will not always be low.

Throughout my working years, I traded my time for money. In order for me to quit working, my money needs to continue to work for me. Possessing enough income and capital is the only difference between a worry-free retirement and a Wal-Mart retirement.

I am getting back on my feet financially. I have always been very good with money—saving and never spending to excess. I have made steady investments in stocks, mutual funds, and in residential investment real estate. I have regularly fed my retirement accounts.

I have worked and trained hard, built a solid work history, and acquired valuable professional skills that are in demand. I had been on track to retire in style at age 53! As it turns out, that was not possible. In a later chapter, I will explain why.

I still work a full-time job. In my free time, I have kicked off a small business with two paths: i) helping people to recover from emotional or financial loss and ii) helping online entrepreneurs to grow their businesses. Now I am back on track to retire soon and independently make all of my financial decisions.

3. My Emotional Profile Today

*"By accepting yourself in the present, you can add to who
you are rather than thinking that you will be OK if
you make certain changes. The difference is powerful."*
— Kristina Von Rosenvinge

I am happy and content. I have healthy relationships with the people in my life. I value others and myself. I appreciate their gifts and diversity. I am more tolerant, am slower to judge than I was in the past, and have more patience than I ever dreamed possible. I now know the boundaries of healthy relationships.

It was much easier to track the progress of my physical and financial recovery than it was to track my emotional recovery because there are fewer outward signs. But now, I have a circle of good friends and acquaintances. I am connected with select family members—some that I had not seen for forty years.

I have people in my circle that I trust, who I can talk to about anything. I know people who are patient, empathetic, and caring. I know people who will cut me some slack when I need it most. I can freely talk to multiple people to obtain several perspectives. I have people in my life who are happy to help me, and I am happy to help them. I am growing better and stronger every day.

I have people in my circle that I trust, who I can talk to about anything.

4. My Spiritual Profile Today

"The possibility of stepping into a higher plane is quite real
for everyone. It requires no force or effort or sacrifice.
It involves little more than changing our ideas about what is normal."
— Deepak Chopra

Today, I am well on my way in my search of a deeper spiritual connection. I am improving in evaluating the choices that I make each day to live out God's purpose. I have enormous gratitude for my blessings and my gifts. I try to see beauty and value in all of God's creations. I am by no means "there" yet, and I am not always successful. But I am working on compassion and avoiding judgments. Now I catch myself faster when I stumble, which is a good sign. I am energized by my spiritual journey, which unfolds before me each day. I do stray; my thoughts go dark. But I bring them back on track, sometimes very quickly. My spiritual journey is empowering and enlightening.

My spiritual journey is empowering and enlightening.

I am involved in a local church community, and I very much enjoy the people there. They are incredibly warm and welcoming. I take part in a weekly Bible study group after the services. It keeps me grounded and connected to God and His Word.

As a critical part of my spiritual journey, I read numerous books including those by Wayne Dyer, Rick Warren, Joyce Meyer, and others (See the Suggested Reading List). I attend the annual Women of Faith conference for Christian inspiration and renewal. I also look for other inspiring messages of faith. I blend the messages from the wide-ranging sources into one message that supports my faith and my life.

Sadly, it wasn't always so. Happily, it is now.

*   *   *   *   *

The next few chapters describe the details of the perfect storm that dominated my life for more than three years. They elaborate on how I lost my mother, my man, my money, and my health—all in a relatively short period. But I survived, and I'll share with you how I did it.

After that, in the next sections, my steps to financial, emotional, and spiritual recovery are presented. The final sections outline a set of five steps (Explore, Eliminate, Embrace, Envision, and Energize) that can guide the recovery of others. Plus, there are some fun quizzes, quotes, and lessons all along the way. So hang on, and enjoy the ride. Here we go.

CHAPTER 2

Our Relationship History

*"By ourselves we can enjoy life, but to really
appreciate life we must find companionship."*
– Anonymous

1. My Career History and Our Relationship

*"And in the end, it's not the years in your life
that count. It's the life in your years."*
– Abraham Lincoln

For almost my entire adult life, my career has been my major focus. I worked, studied, morphed, clawed, and climbed my way up; in doing so, I gave up any semblance of a normal life. I was determined that where I finished would not be limited by where I started.

In my early days, my father instilled in me the message that girls would never amount to anything and that college was a waste of time for women. He even tried to block my student loan, but thankfully, my mother intervened on my behalf. I only realize now how much my mother loved me and how courageous she was to be my sole advocate against my father's repressive views. With my mother's intervention I was able to secure a student loan for my undergraduate study successfully; and I paid it back in full six months after graduation.

From then on, I set out to prove my father wrong. And prove him wrong I did. I was a classic workaholic with an addictive personality. As it turns out, this lifestyle choice filled both my emotional and financial needs. What could possibly be wrong with that? To achieve a good career, I paid a huge price.

To achieve a good career, I paid a huge price. I had no friends and no family connections to speak of besides my mother—no balance in my life whatsoever.

Retirement, getting out of the rat race, became my primary goal; it was my dream, my hope, and my symbol of victory. I yearned for the time when I wouldn't have to be so driven, ferocious, and competitive. I wanted to stop fighting and swimming with the sharks. My plan was to retire at age 53; that sounds like an early age to retire, but measured in billable hours I was actually 62! I worked it all out and began to position myself financially. Over the years, I built up a nice nest egg, bought residential investment properties, and arranged for long-term care and retiree medical insurance. Throughout this time, I continued to work, study, and save. The month before I met John (who would eventually become my fiancé) in 1988, I had just started a seven-year Ph.D. program while working full time—well, make that working *more* than full time.

In the only way that I knew how, I worked and worked to try to increase my perceived value in my own mind. My dad taught me that women had no value, so I was out there in the man's world engaged in commerce; I was not at home ironing as he predicted. But success in business went hand-in-hand with great sacrifices in my personal life.

I used my career to try to fulfill my emotional needs—looking outside myself toward an external source. I felt good about myself through my professional accomplishments.

From the age of twenty-eight to fifty-three, I was almost 100% focused on my career and getting ahead. I never—ever—considered having children; there was just no time. Plus I did not have the desire or the courage to bring children into this world. Anyway, all that mattered to me was my career. I tried to prove my value based on my father's model—by making money. I guess I tried to earn some recognition of my value and seek the approval that I never received growing up.

For one 18-month stretch I commuted to New York City every week. As my work schedule was very unpredictable, it was difficult to plan activities after work. Many days I had very little energy left anyway. I had to participate in lots of overtime, last-minute meetings that changed my plans, and much travel. I can't even estimate how many plans I cancelled due to unexpected work commitments popping up at the last minute. But, through it all, I was doing it. I reached the level of Director in PricewaterhouseCoopers Consulting—not bad at all for a girl from a backward blue-collar family. *So there, take that!* I thought.

On a parallel track, in my personal life, my companionship with John was absolutely what I needed to get through those incredible work and PhD-study years. John and I were together every weekend that I was in town. Sometimes, especially in the early years, we would also go out dancing in the middle of the week; it did not matter what time we arrived at the club, so dancing was a good low-stress and fun activity for both of us. We always had a great time together.

2. His Career History and Our Relationship

*"It is every man's obligation to put back into the world
at least the equivalent of what he takes out of it."*
– Albert Einstein

Over the same 16 years, John totally focused on paying expenses for his ex-wife and their children. He paid twelve years of tuition in private colleges for his three kids after paying for years and years of private schools. He also paid his ex-wife a seven-year property settlement. In addition, he bought out his business partner over ten years. As a result, he worked very hard but had little leftover cash to show for it due to his extensive family and business obligations. He paid and paid and paid, and he really made great headway. Time was on his side. He was truly getting ahead a little at a time.

He decided that his three kids would come out of college with zero debt, an incredible goal. I was proud that he fulfilled the commitments that he had chosen to make to his family. I thought that it showed strong character on his part. Our companion relationship met his needs very well for 16 years. He focused on his business and his family commitments. And every weekend, we'd go out on the town.

His move to Florida in 2004 meant that this was the beginning of our time. It was finally happening. At last, his responsibilities had been fulfilled. He had worked so hard and accomplished so much. And now, he deserved to live the good life in retirement.

This would be the first time since we met in 1988 that he would have a little financial breathing room—finally. The man had fully paid the expenses of five people for years and years, and they were now all finally living independently without his support. I don't know how he did it; it was truly admirable but a long slog, nonetheless. And there were many lean years along the way.

3. Our Plans Together

"The most important thing in life is to learn how
to give out love, and to let it come in."
– Morrie Schwartz

In the early days of our relationship, things were great. John was kind, intelligent, caring, supportive, and lots of fun. And he danced; it is rare to find a man who danced, but I found one. He was a gentleman who opened doors for me. I knew his parents very well and they made every effort to raise their sons with honor, as gentlemen. They *I was so thrilled to* believed that the actions that their sons took *have found a gentleman.* reflected on the entire family so the sons were advised to keep their actions above reproach. I was so thrilled to have found a gentleman. He accompanied me to office parties, and I accompanied him. We had a lot of fun together; we were constant companions on the weekends; we either ate out or he cooked for us. He changed his golf plans to play at 7 a.m. so that we could have Sunday afternoons and evenings together. We loved each other very much; we were ideal soul mates.

John worked very hard himself so he readily accepted my extensive work and travel schedule. He put up with me complaining about the dramas and politics at work. He helped me move five times. Sometimes, as a favor to me, John would even stay at my house to cat sit while I was away, and my beloved cat, Katie, loved every minute of it.

So as it turned out, the long-term companion arrangement truly met both of our needs perfectly. As he approached his final payments, he cut back on working hours, played a lot more golf, and prepared to sell his business so he could retire and start a new life—with me.

...the long-term companion arrangement truly met both of our needs perfectly.

We provided moral support for each other when the winds of change blew and the seas were stormy. Of course, the relationship would've never lasted so long if we hadn't done so.   Being companions was fine for the first 16 years, but we both knew that we could be so much more. Throughout this time, we had never lived together. This was truly a new beginning for us as a "real" couple. I envisioned us as being very, very happy together in our new life.

Being companions was fine for the first 16 years, but we both knew that we could be so much more.

His past was behind him, and our future was ahead of us. We became engaged and proceeded with plans to sell his business and solidify my retirement.

CHAPTER 3

Elder Care Crisis with My Mother

"Respect for one's parents is the highest duty..."
– Chinese proverb

1. First Signs of Trouble

I gradually took over my mother's financial affairs after my father died in 1999; at that time, my parents had already been in Florida for more than fifteen years. I was pleasantly surprised by her financial position and her investment holdings. She was in good financial shape other than having too many telecom stocks. All was in order; even her house was paid for. Even without my father's income, my mother was able to maintain her lifestyle without any changes—what a relief that was.

Although my mother endured a rocky fifty-four-year marriage with a repressive, controlling husband, she was happy and reasonably healthy when I assumed coordination of her finances. Bring on the bingo, line dancing, crafts, cards, and shopping for bargains for the church! She

Bring on the bingo, line dancing, crafts, cards...

collected bags, boxes, and snap tops. You name it and she collected it. Her sun porch was filled with huge quantities of stuff. She was very happy and in her element, helping others in every way she could.

My Mother Can't Remember

For a couple of years after my father's death, my mother was very active—coming and going all the time. Then gradually, her memory started to fade—just a little at first. However, it became more noticeable and troublesome. She would drive to the store and would not be able to remember how to get home. Mild dementia had taken root, and unfortunately, continuing to drive risked her safety and security. And believe me; this on-the-go woman did not want to give up her license!

The Neighbor as a Guardian Angel

Enter her next-door neighbor, an incredible gentleman who offered to drive her wherever she wanted to go. Looking back now, this man was an angel on earth. He took her grocery shopping. He made sure that she ate every day. He took her to the doctor. He managed her medications. One of her medications was Coumadin, a powerful blood thinner, which necessitated frequent blood checks. My mother's neighbor did an excellent job keeping her in good health on Coumadin for more than 18 months. In a word, he was amazing. And he would not accept payment for this enormous favor that he did for her.

With his help, my mother held on to her independence even as she slowly lost her cognitive abilities. Fortunately, my mother could still walk to many activities in the community. This was an ideal arrangement as her favorite activities (bingo and crafts) were still readily accessible to her. She kept very busy and weathered this period quite well.

Even with such good care, I knew there would come a time when her helpful neighbor could no longer care for her.

Even with such good care, I knew there would come a time when her helpful neighbor could no longer care for her. So, my fiancé had the inspired idea to very subtly start to scout for assisted living facilities in advance. We'd drive by them and ask what she thought about each facility and whether she knew anyone who lived there. Several ladies from her community were in a certain facility that she liked the best. We looked at a few other facilities just for comparison. We duly noted where my mother preferred to go when it was time, not knowing that the time was almost upon us.

2. The Move to Assisted Living

The day had come when my mother's angel neighbor could no longer handle all of her needs. Actually, that day had long passed, but I was unaware of it. In basic conversations, my mother had become a master at fooling people into thinking that she was on top of things. She could converse well, and people would always underestimate the extent of her dementia.

…my mother had become a master at fooling people into thinking that she was on top of things.

Even though her neighbor thought the move was long overdue, some of her friends thought that I was jumping the gun—well in advance of her need to move into assisted living. In fact, one of her best bingo buddies who picked her up every Friday night scolded me for acting prematurely. She was very sure that my mother was okay. But that was not the case.

So on to assisted living it was. (Follow along with the timeline in the appendix.) At the facility, there were several levels of care. Based on my mother's needs, we selected Assisted Living Level 2. With the AL2 level of service, my mother had a small private apartment. The staff would check in on her regularly and escort her to the dining hall and beauty salon if needed. They would also escort her to the doctor, and administer and monitor her prescribed medications. All was well.

When I was not traveling for work, I would visit every other weekend and take her to the grocery store so that she had those little extras that make life special. At the AL facility, she had full meal service, but the breakfast schedule was too early for my mother, the night owl. When we went out, she bought juice, cereal, milk, and some candy and ice cream. Little special things meant a lot to her and gave her a feeling of independence and joy.

All was well for a while.

3. The Medical Error that Changed Everything

Only five months after the move into the assisted living facility, the trouble began. One morning at work, I received a call from the facility telling me that my mother looked purple. I immediately said, "Hang up the phone and call 911 right away; it's probably the Coumadin." The attendant said that she was not sure what it was. Then, I repeated with more intensity, "Hang up now and call 911."

My mother was bleeding under her skin—a very serious matter indeed. Her clotting time was not checked as prescribed after her Coumadin dosage was adjusted. Apparently, the doctor gave verbal orders to the escort as well as faxed the written orders to the facility's medical unit. Her Coumadin dosage had been changed, and my mother needed to be re-tested after two weeks. But somehow, both of those messages were lost in the shuffle.

My mother was rushed to the emergency room. It was very, very serious. She was eighty years old, suffering from Alzheimer's, and was now the victim of a medical error on top of it—the poor woman. I jumped on a plane to be by her side. It was touch and go for quite a while. I thought I was going to lose her, the situation was so serious. They worked on her for almost two weeks in the ICU to stabilize her condition, to bring her blood levels back in line, and to revive her systems.

I felt completely helpless and powerless. I did not know what else to do, so I prayed. And I prayed some more.

It was during this very troubling time that I found a path back to my faith. I learned to pray. I felt completely helpless and powerless. I did not know what else to do, so I prayed. And I prayed some more. Then, there was a ray of hope.

Unbelievably, my mother improved and eventually was considered well enough to be transferred to a skilled nursing facility for physical rehabilitation. My mother had endured quite a lot. Her system had been poisoned with an overdose of blood thinner. But she fought back. What a trouper she was. She had gone for weeks without walking, and her muscles lacked strength, but nonetheless, this was a very positive development in her recovery.

Not long after she arrived at the skilled nursing facility, another unrelated medical problem surfaced, and my mother returned to the hospital. After a second brief stint in the hospital, my mother was released again and sent back to the skilled nursing facility to restart her physical rehabilitation. After a brave and committed struggle in rehab, she returned to her apartment in the assisted living facility under 24-hour supervision. Ah, peace and quiet with no 6:30 a.m. wake-ups to take a pill—all was well. She was back in her own bed with no tubes, no noise, and no interruptions from a clinical setting.

It appeared that my mother had survived this very serious medical error. *Thank God for her improving health*, I thought. Perhaps she could once again begin to enjoy her retirement in peace in a warm, stable, non-clinical living environment. Sadly, it was not to be. Not long after she returned to the assisted living facility and the facility removed the 24-hour companion, my mother blacked out and was found on the floor of her apartment. She was rushed to the ER. This took a very heavy toll on her. Perhaps she had never fully recovered from the medical error after all. Maybe she needed much more care than was being provided. This all happened so fast—one crisis right after the other.

4. The Medical Runaround—Take One

From the ER, she was moved to the ICU where she stayed for weeks. Some of the same medical staff who had cared for my mother in her earlier admissions to the ICU attended to her needs once again. Some of the ICU medical staff were nice and gave my mother compassionate care beyond what was required. But some of them were impatient with both my mother and me. I remember calling the ICU nurse on Thanksgiving morning in 2005 to inquire about my mother's condition. The nurse implied that my mother could die at any minute. I asked if I should drop everything and make the two-hour drive from my house in Florida to get to the hospital right away even though I was hosting a holiday dinner for eight. She said to wait an hour and call the other ICU nurse. I was very worried. My mother could die at any minute, and there I was cooking sweet potatoes! *What on earth am I doing?* I wondered.

The nurse implied that my mother could die at any minute.

An hour later, the other ICU nurse was very compassionate and indicated that my mother was stable and sedated, that the ventilator was doing all the work, and that I should not worry. She told me that I should enjoy my holiday plans and visit the next day. What an emotional trip—in one hour, the message evolved from my mother being near imminent death to it being no big deal at all; tomorrow would be fine.

It is difficult to be efficient or effective when it comes to elder care.

It is difficult to be efficient or effective when it comes to elder care. Anyone who has done it knows what I mean. I am accustomed to solving problems. I can research facts, array the options, calculate the probabilities, and find the optimal solution; I can be effective. I can be efficient. But none of that matters when it comes to elder care.

The next day I visited my mother for a few hours, and one of the doctors asked me if my mother had a DNR (a DNR is a Do Not Resuscitate order that allows paramedics and hospital staff to legally withhold CPR and other aggressive life-saving measures from patients with poor prognoses). The doctor indicated that he thought that my mother's condition was hopeless. *Oh!* I thought, *I didn't realize we were there yet*. Apparently, the medical error had sapped her strength and stripped her resilience. This was far worse than I had feared; I had gotten my hopes up when she appeared to recover the last time.

This was far worse than I had feared; I had gotten my hopes up when she appeared to recover the last time.

I knew that my mother had a living will stipulating to remove life support if her condition became hopeless. But at the time, I did not know the distinction between the living will (removing care) and the DNR (withholding care). The doctor wanted to withhold CPR in the event of an episode of heart failure. I said that I did not know about the existence of a DNR but that, as her medical representative, I would look into it.

"I am still here. I can hear you."

The doctor scowled and walked away muttering to himself and to an ICU nurse standing nearby about me and all those other adult children who do not adhere to the legal directives of their parents. I clearly told him that I did not know about a DNR and that I would look into it. As he walked away ridiculing me, I called out to the doctor, "I am still here. I can hear you." I am a reasonably successful, well-educated businessperson. I have been in hundreds of professional situations, but this doctor treated me like a complete idiot.

The hospital staff that see older people taking up critical-care beds often refer to them as GOMERs, which stands for "Get Out of My Emergency Room." In this case, it was the ICU, but the same principle applies. My mother was hanging in there but was now considered by some to be a GOMER. A chronically ill senior does not belong in the ICU. Some on the medical team found it hard to hide their disdain for the ongoing situation. But my mother could not be moved to a regular hospital ward while she was hooked to a ventilator. She was in medical no man's land.

She's Getting Better

I have never in my life been on such an emotional roller coaster. I only wanted to do what was best for my mother—just like anyone else would in the same situation. But the question lingered: Could she indeed get better? Some doctors said no way. Other doctors instructed me not to give up hope.

Amazingly, to the disbelief of some of the medical team and especially the doctor who derided me about the DNR, my mother was eventually able to breathe on her own without the ventilator. She had been heavily sedated so it was impossible to assess what she was capable of doing on her own. Soon thereafter, she was released from the hospital and sent to a skilled nursing facility to start physical rehabilitation, yet again. After a couple of weeks, she returned to her apartment in the assisted living facility. *What a relief*, I thought. We had truly dodged another crisis.

Not For Long

Even though my mother had a 24-hour companion by her side, she still fell. Apparently, the aide wrongly assumed that my mother did not need help in the bathroom. My mother fell in the worst possible room in the apartment with extremely hard surfaces all around. She hurt her back and was rushed to the hospital. But nothing showed up on the x-rays. My mother was discharged back to assisted living facility with the 24-hour companion by her side. My mother may not have broken any bones, but she was in extreme pain.

She fell two more times, and I couldn't take it any longer. I clearly believed that this facility could no longer responsibly take care of my *She fell two more times, and I couldn't take it any longer.*

mother given her current condition. She was still in a severely weakened state that we assumed was due to the medical error. Her decline in health had been remarkable since she left her home. When she first entered the facility, she was an active, vibrant, energetic, and happy senior. Then the medical error set the stage for her precipitous and irreversible deterioration.

Move to a Higher Level of Care

After much searching and negotiation over a period of several days, I moved my mother back to the skilled nursing facility that had given her excellent rehab care. My fiancé helped enormously; John played a very active role in the negotiations and scheduling and helped to keep me relatively calm through all of this. His support was critical in keeping me held together during this time of rolling and repetitive crises.

It was a major achievement to move her back into that skilled nursing facility. They were short of beds, and there was a long waiting list. But because my mother had just been there, she was moved to the top of the list. However, we still had to wait for a bed to free up. I constantly tried to do what was best for my mother, and this looked like the best move given her severely weakened condition. In just a few days, a bed became available, and my mother was moved back to this excellent skilled nursing facility to receive a level of care that the assisted living facility could not provide.

Finally, my mother was being appropriately cared for in the proper facility. This setting was clinical, not residential, so the 24-hour companion sat directly beside my mother's hospital bed; there was no way she could fall now. I tried so hard to do the right thing. It looked like all the hard work had paid off. Relief flooded through me. She was in the right place for her needs.

It looked like all the hard work had paid off.

She stayed there one day. Yes, one day.

Back to the Hospital

After one day in the skilled nursing facility, my mother became "unresponsive" and was sent back to the ER. She was quickly moved to the ICU and put back on a ventilator. *How could this possibly happen?* I questioned. *Everything was going so well.* My poor mother was experiencing a living hell.

This time, the situation looked very grim. These repeated relapses were a very bad sign. She had no awareness of her surroundings and was back on that ventilator, which was so uncomfortable. Her lips were dry and cracked; she was thirsty all the time. This lasted for weeks until she could no longer be on a ventilator due to the pressure of the mouthpiece on her throat.

One doctor believed that she could improve with a tracheotomy—that is, surgery on an eighty-one-year-old Alzheimer's patient who was still trying to recover fully from the earlier medical error. Others were quite skeptical and thought that there was no hope whatsoever.

Just when it was time to resign myself to the fact that the situation was hopeless, my mother regained awareness. Everyone stopped talking about removing life support. Amazingly, she kept bouncing back.

My mother continued to gradually improve so the decision was made by the medical team to schedule a tracheotomy. There is a physical limit to how long a patient can be on a ventilator. The tubes rub on the back of the throat and

There is a physical limit to how long a patient can be on a ventilator.

cause abrasions; so at some point, the tubes must be removed. The end-of-life decisions that were relevant just days before were apparently no longer relevant, but surgery was.

However, problematically, with a tracheotomy, my mother would need constant care, which was too long term for the ICU and too advanced for the regular hospital ward. Consequently, she was transferred via ambulance to a teaching hospital two hours away where patients with tracheotomies received specialized care. There she would also obtain advanced care to boost her respiratory capacity so that she could breathe on her own.

This teaching hospital had been known to work wonders on patients with serious respiratory difficulties. I was cautiously optimistic that her respiratory difficulties could indeed be remedied. I went along with the recommendations of the medical team.

This had all been very taxing on an eighty-one-year old woman with dementia.

After two weeks and a battery of tests, the new medical team indicated that there was no hope for my mother to reliably breathe on her own. She had been severely weakened by the medical error and all of the subsequent episodes and interventions. This had all been very taxing on an eighty-one-year old woman with dementia.

By March 2006, it was time for the decision. I only wanted what was best for my mother. Her quality of life was nonexistent. So with much sadness, I circulated the paperwork to my two brothers to authorize the removal of the life support. My brothers, who were mostly absent and uninvolved during this entire saga, finally came to visit my mother after my urgent plea; they agreed to the decision. Still trying to do the best thing for my mother and do what she would have wanted, my dear mother—my friend, companion, and champion against my father's gender prejudice—was taken off life support.

May God rest her soul.

The Year in Review

After nearly a year in and out of five facilities with constantly changing conditions, prognoses, levels of care, and degrees of compassion from the medical team, the time had arrived. Looking back, I know that I did the best I could and made the best decisions with what I knew at the time. My mother lived a long and full life. That gave me some comfort—to the extent that is even possible with the protracted suffering and loss of a parent. My heart goes out to all who have lost loved ones. I am truly sorry for your loss. But even through the darkness there is hope and help.

I learned that when faced with conflicting opinions, it was important to talk to family. It was much easier to handle all of the swirling emotions when all of the facts and opinions were on the table.

My fiancé helped me enormously in sorting through all of the facility decisions. It was truly a comfort to have him at my side. My fiancé also assisted me enormously at my mother's funeral. He kept me glued together; he was my rock. I loved him so much.

CHAPTER 4

Real Estate Investment as a Placeholder

"...Put your money in land, because they aren't making any more of it."
–Will Rogers

1. Pre-Retirement Planning

I am seven years behind the leading edge of the boomers. Looking into the future, a vast number of baby boomers would be retiring ahead of me. It seems funny now, but I thought that I should find a placeholder property in a desirable retirement community so that when I did settle on my final retirement home, I would be able to afford the future climbing prices through the sale of the placeholder property. You know, supply and demand. I had a charming residential investment property in Santa Barbara that had appreciated nicely, so it was time to do a tax-free exchange into another residential investment property.

In March 2003, I began looking, with John in tow, in South Carolina and in Florida. I loved Hilton Head, SC, but John thought Florida would be the best placeholder because he was preparing to sell his business—approximately 1.5 years before my target retirement date. He wanted to take advantage of a 10 percent savings in state income tax on the upcoming sale of his business. If his business sold as part of an installment sale, he might have to stay in Florida for several more years to get the full benefit of living in an income tax-free state. We

We agreed that we could move anywhere after the income tax implications from the sale of his business, his single largest asset, were settled.

agreed that we could move anywhere after the income tax implications from the sale of his business, his single largest asset, were settled.

Over a ten-day period, we took a whirlwind tour through northern, central, and western Florida and found one community on the east coast and one on the west coast that might serve as good placeholders. The quality of the golf course was an important consideration in rising property values, so I purchased a lot in the community on the west coast with the better golf course. I hoped that solid price appreciation would be ahead of the inevitable influx of retiring boomers. It seemed like a great placeholder. The Santa Barbara house sold quickly, and I proceeded with the tax-free exchange.

The lot I selected backed up to a lagoon in a nice country club community that had a premium golf course along the river. But it did not have things that I thought were important attributes for my retirement community, such as tennis courts, a nice dance floor in the party room, a separate activities center, and mature hardwood trees. *Not to worry,* I thought, because it was only a placeholder property after all. It did not need to meet my specific needs. I felt no pressure to make a major decision; there would be time to do an extended search for an ideal retirement house in the perfect retirement community later. And, I believed, the search itself would be a lot of fun.

I felt no pressure to make a major decision; there would be time to do an extended search for an ideal retirement house in the perfect retirement community later.

The developer planned to build fairly soon. This schedule helped me to capture the full benefits of the 1031 exchange, so I signed on. My realtor said that it would be no problem to find tenants to move into my house while I did the countdown to my retirement date. The best chance was for seven to eight-month rentals from couples who were building houses in the community and had already sold their houses up north.

Couples who were building preferred to rent in the same community to start to make new connections and friends. And they had housefuls of furniture so they would be perfect tenants for a new, unfurnished house. She estimated that two tenants would nicely cover the period up until my planned retirement date.

Because it was to be a rental, I felt very reluctant to have a pool installed. There are sobering statistics of children drowning in pools so I thought a rental house with a pool would be a nightmare. In fact, in one of my investment properties in California I had a pool removed for that very reason. But the realtor informed me that 97 percent of the houses in the community had a pool, so my house would be at a severe market disadvantage if it did not have one. I asked about adding a pool later when it was time to sell or giving the buyer a pool credit, but I was told that the price would be very high for a much lower-quality pool. Indeed, the best time to add a pool was when the house was being built, not after. So I agreed to put in a pool to ensure that the house was marketable. As a placeholder, it definitely needed to be a desirable property in the community.

2. The Unlikely Tenant

When the house was halfway built, John indicated that he would like to rent my house. I could not believe it; the house was 2,500 square feet and had four bedrooms and three baths along with a living room, dining room, family room, eat-in kitchen, and large pool deck. What would he possibly do with a house that size by himself? I was still working full time 1,000 miles away.

Even as long-time companions, sixteen years at that time, we had never had any serious business dealings with each other, so I was reluctant to start before we got our finances sorted out and we were married. And the house was so big and empty.

He had no viable furniture; he was jettisoning the old mismatched bachelor stuff he had in his house up north. He said not to worry about it. And he knew that I was concerned about the pool liability. He said that he needed a Florida address and that I needed a tenant, so it worked out well for both of us—a real win-win situation. I relented to his persuasive pleadings. He always could win me over with his petitions. It seemed to make sense, and it was only a lease after all.

We were both very reasonable. We were experienced and savvy businesspeople. We loved each other very much. We got along great—better than any other couple we knew. What could possibly go wrong with a lease that

What could possibly go wrong with a lease that we couldn't work out?

we couldn't work out? It sounded logical, so I agreed to let him rent my house instead of renting to couples who were building in the community.

We worked out rent at $2,000 a month plus pool service expenses on a one-year lease starting in December 2003. And I had locking pool doors installed so that no one could enter the pool area from the outside. John agreed to keep the pool fence up when he was away. These safety precautions relieved my major concerns. He gradually moved in while preparing his house for sale up north, which was quite an ordeal because significant repairs were needed.

A few months after he moved in, it became apparent that he loved the house and the community. He made dozens of friends on the golf course; he played golf twice a day. Yes, that is not a typo; he played golf twice a day on most days.

He furnished the house with a queen bed, a twenty-inch TV, and the two camping chairs the realtor had given me as a welcoming gift—very sparse furnishings in a 2,500 sq ft. house. He pleaded that we stay in the house and give it a try as "our" house so that he could buy nice furniture instead of wasting money on cheap temporary furniture.

The people in the community were very nice and friendly—not what I had feared in a "frou-frou" country club community. I'd made a few friends just by visiting every other weekend when I flew down. I agreed to give it a try for a little while, even though it did not have tennis facilities, my primary recreational activity. I was hoping to move to Hilton Head, SC after the tax implications of selling his business were sorted out.

Based on my agreement to give the house a try, starting in May 2004, he bought approximately $50,000 in nice furniture and accessories for the entire house. His kids and grandkids would be the most frequent users of the guest bedrooms, so a set of twin beds and a queen bed were part of his furnishings.

3. The Six Happiest Months of My Life

The next six months were the happiest time of my life. For the previous sixteen years, we had only been close companions. We were now engaged and began to plan our new life together in earnest. We shopped all over the area for an eclectic blend of contemporary furniture, and I started to decorate the house. It was so much fun.

There was finally an "us." It was truly amazing. I was ecstatic that this was finally going to be our time. We had both worked so hard for so long. He had made sure that his kids were equipped to fly solo. There was finally going to be a time for us as a couple. I was so happy. I felt so secure. I couldn't imagine feeling any happier than I felt at the time. It was truly an amazing six months—indeed, the happiest time of my life.

> *I was ecstatic that this was finally going to be our time. We had both worked so hard for so long.*

But alas, this intense happiness did not last.

4. It Costs How Much?

In November 2004, I received the first property tax bill for the house. It was $12,000. Shocked, I thought, *Oh my goodness! How is this possible?* The house value had increased considerably from when I bought it; and before that, it was taxed as a vacant lot. I had previously owned investment properties in Virginia, Maryland, California, and South Carolina—and most recently in Florida. I have never seen a property tax bill of this magnitude in twenty-five years of owning residential investment properties. So, as it turns out, the downside of having no state income taxes in Florida is the sky-high property taxes. But I was in a very unusual situation; I was still paying income taxes in my home state *and* sky-high property taxes in Florida. It was

> *It was the worst of both worlds for me.*

the worst of both worlds for me. But it was the best of both worlds for John; he paid neither state income taxes nor property taxes.

Not only was there a huge property tax liability on the house, but there were also a myriad of other extremely high annual expenses as well, such as the following:

$12,000	property taxes
$2,400	property insurance
$2,100	homeowners association

$2,000	supplies
$1,800	grass cutting
$1,200	pool maintenance
$1,000	tree and shrub treatments
$500	termite control
$500	pest control
$500	lawn treatments
$24,000	estimated annual expenses

It was quite an impressive list of fixed costs—and there were other costs as well. Plus, we did the actual weeding and gardening ourselves. Many times, my every-other-weekend visits to the property would turn into weed-pulling and shrub-trimming festivals. What a hoot!

The soil in the lot had been dredged off the bottom of the lagoon behind the house and thus contained zero nutrients. Everything needed to be fed all the time. There was no actual soil to speak of—only barren sand. The weeds, alone, loved it. And the pests—they were everywhere: bugs of all shapes and sizes and squirrels in the attic. The upkeep of this house was very, very high indeed.

It cost $24,000 a year to simply maintain a paid-off house! That did not include utilities or repairs. That did not count food, clothing, health insurance, cars, gas, car insurance, and other expenses that retirees on fixed incomes need to fund.

We planned to retire "comfortably" but were by no means rich. I considered the ongoing costs of maintaining this house in retirement utterly ridiculous. Worse yet, what would inflation do to these numbers over time? This house was way too expensive to retire in. I told *...what would inflation do to these numbers over time?* John what I thought, but he disagreed. The seeds of discontent were starting to emerge. He didn't think it was that expensive given how nice the community was. This was the first indication of major trouble; I just didn't realize it at the time. The dialogue went on for a year until September 2005 when it was time for me to begin the retirement process.

CHAPTER 5

Unbelievable Betrayal

*"Trust is like a vase… once it's broken, though you
can fix it the vase will never be the same again."*
– George MacDonald

1. My Retirement Date Is Here

In the cruelest of coincidences my retirement date coincided perfectly with the final stages of my mother's advancing illness. In November 2005, I qualified for retiree medical coverage—a major milestone in my life and financial planning. *Lucky me!* I thought, *I am fifty-three, and my retirement date is here.* After thirty-eight years of working nights, weekends, fifty-sixty-hour weeks, and traveling all over the world, it was finally time for me to retire early. What a lifetime achievement—especially considering where I started from!

After changing jobs multiple times to find better opportunities and to advance my career, my final job would provide me with retiree medical coverage before the age of sixty-five when Medicare kicked in. This was amazing; I had never expected such an incredible benefit. But now that I had it, I was certainly going to take full advantage of it.

I could not believe it was now time to actually put my retirement wheels in motion. Unbelievably, things were working out just as I had planned. Yes, hard work does pay. Only in America could the female child of a backward

> *I could not believe it was now time to actually put my retirement wheels in motion.*

blue-collar family reach these heights. It was time to sell my house. It was time for him to sell his business. This was it—finally!

Except, it wasn't.

During the previous year, he had made no progress selling his business, which was the only reason for him to move to Florida ahead of me in the first place. Sure, he had chatted with a few prospects here and there. But as it turned out, he was not in any particular hurry to sell it after all. But now, with my retirement date upon us, it was time for him to try to sell it in earnest.

Except, it wasn't.

I inquired about John's progress in selling his business because my retirement date was approaching fast. Somewhere along the line at an unknown point in time, he decided that he was not going to sell his business after all. He did not believe that, as his fiancée, I needed to be informed of his decision.

What? He had moved one thousand miles away from me expressly to sell his business, and now he was not going to sell it. For about 18 months from April 2004 to September 2005, we each flew back and forth every other weekend because he decided to move to Florida to sell his business. We spent thousands of dollars in airfare—plus just on my end, I drove fifty miles to the airport after work every other Thursday in rush-hour traffic, not to mention airport parking and gas. And he was doing the same—except with no rush hour in Florida.

I wasted huge amounts of time waiting ninety minutes at the airport and two hours on planes each way with delays and waits in TSA lines, shoeless, with my cosmetics stuffed into those familiar one-quart clear zipper bags, just so he could sell his business from Florida. Now he had unilaterally decided that he was not selling his business and that it was not even sufficiently important enough news for him to share his decision with me. I was very concerned. Didn't he need to diversify? What if something happened in the marketplace? What if something happened to his key staff? How could we buy a house together if all of his money was still tied up in the business?

How could we buy a house together if all of his money was still tied up in the business?

In parallel, as my planned retirement date approached, I informed him that it was time for me to sell my house. Amazingly, after some capital improvements increased the base value, the house had appreciated from what I paid (about $500,000) to approximately $725,000—what a great gain in 2.5 years. This was exactly what the placeholder property was designed to do. It was time to cash in just in time for my retirement. Even though it was a nice house in a nice community with friendly people, the house was just too expensive for retirement. We had "discussed" the details for nearly a year by then. I had way too much of my retirement money tied up; I wanted my capital out. Even if it had been feasible to stay there, he had no funds to buy half of the house anyway because he had no intention of selling his business.

After all, it was just a placeholder that I purchased as part of a 1031 exchange from my Santa Barbara investment property. The community had no tennis courts, no activities center, and a very small dance floor—key attributes that I would be looking for in a retirement community. Yes, I agreed to give this house a try. And I did give it a try. But I had not realized how extremely expensive that house would be to maintain. I believed that it was unsuitable for retirement.

But he loved that house more than anything on the face of the earth—and he was determined to stay.

But he loved that house more than anything on the face of the earth—and he was determined to stay. He decided that I would not sell my house. Sure, I was the one with a lot of capital at risk. Actually, he had no capital in danger. A listing of $725,000 would be expected to net about $650,000. That was my retirement money in jeopardy; he only had $50,000 "invested" in furniture that would move with us anyway.

...he placed our relationship in jeopardy for a house—my house.

He vehemently objected to me selling my house—over and over. How is it possible for someone to control a $725,000 house when he only contributed $2,000 a month in rent? It was simply outrageous. Who would do something so low as to highjack his fiancée's house when her mother was dying? I was not prepared for a full-on battle with John at that time. I was absolutely not ready to put our long-term relationship on the line for a house, but apparently he was. I just could not believe the situation. After all that we had been through together and all of the plans that we made, he placed our relationship in jeopardy for a house—my house.

2. The Betrayal

When my retirement date arrived, my fiancé was renting my house and had no intention of moving out. I never imagined he would be so unreasonable, especially when my mother was dying. He had been with me through thick

I honestly must say that I was at my limit for crises. and thin. He was well aware that I was emotionally frazzled, beginning with my mother's Alzheimer's diagnosis. Then the medical error compounded the problem and rapidly accelerated her decline. I honestly

must say that I was at my limit for crises. We were only barely engaged, but how had he already decided that he was in control of me and my money? The time had come to truly sort this out. I calmly opened the discussion.

DONNA MARIE: "My retirement is here. It's time for me to sell the house."

JOHN: "You're not selling this house!"

DONNA MARIE: "But this house is really expensive."

JOHN: "No, it's not."

DONNA MARIE: "The taxes are really high."

JOHN: "No, they're not."

DONNA MARIE: "I need the money from the house to retire."

JOHN: "No, you don't. You've got plenty of other money."

DONNA MARIE: "Yes, I really do need the money from this house to retire."

JOHN: "No, you don't. You've got more money than most people in this community."

DONNA MARIE: "What are you talking about?"

JOHN: "Never mind. I don't want to talk about this. You are upsetting me. You are not selling this house!"

I didn't know what had just happened. What was going on here? He used to be reasonable. Now he was vehement. *How can he not realize that a lot of my retirement money is tied up in this house?* I wondered. By this time, we had been together for

This person that I planned to spend the rest of my life with had turned into a selfish, belligerent concrete block.

seventeen years. Often we said the same thing at the same time. We played golf and tennis together. We danced, kayaked, biked, and skated together. We did everything together. We got along great. We laughed and hardly ever had a disagreement. What was going on? This person that I planned to spend the rest of my life with had turned into a selfish, belligerent concrete block. *Wait a minute*, I thought. *This can't be my fiancé, this must be an imposter. How did an imposter enter into our special relationship without me noticing?* I did not understand. After all, he often said that I was the woman of his dreams. Would someone, anyone, please tell me what is happening? I was in no way prepared for his selfishness and viciousness. I could not even believe that this was the same person. Where was the gentleman that I had known and loved for so long?

Time ticked away, and my retirement date arrived, but my major focus was on arranging quality care for my mother to address her rapidly increasing needs. I tried and tried to come up with new ways to convey my point to John. I could list the house for $725,000—it was time to go, to take the money and run.

3. Too Much for Me at the Same Time

Now if these were normal times, I would have simply put the house on the market and given him the choice to either move out right away or to stay in the house while it was on the market. The tenant has no right to block the owner from selling a property. I tried and tried to relay the key points. But nothing worked. And these were not normal times.

Breathing only through the assistance of a ventilator, my mother was in the ICU on her deathbed. I was totally tied up with arranging her care and repeatedly moving her in and out of assisted living, skilled nursing, and hospital facilities. John was quite supportive and helpful in my efforts with my mother but was intransigent when it came to letting go of my house.

I tried to think of what I could possibly say that would convince him to let go of my house. But he vehemently objected to selling the home. I didn't understand how he thought he could just take over my house. He had ZERO equity in the property. *What is going on?* I pondered.

Then I thought that maybe he was upset because he went out and bought nice furniture thinking that we were going to stay in the house for quite a while. In the following conversation, I tried to allay that concern:

DONNA MARIE: "I will buy the furniture from you."

JOHN: "You're not taking the furniture!"

He blocked me from selling my house and proceeding with my retirement plans. All the while, my mother was dying. But he wouldn't listen to me. Instead, he mocked and ridiculed me.

DONNA MARIE: "I need the money from the house to retire."

JOHN: "You've got plenty of other money."

DONNA MARIE: "Yeah, right. I've got an extra $650,000 right here in my back pocket."

***** More ridicule. More blocks. *****

DONNA MARIE: "I need to sell this house to retire."

JOHN: "Don't bring this subject up again."

DONNA MARIE: "But I need the money to retire."

JOHN: "No, you don't."

DONNA MARIE: "Why can't I talk about *my* house?"

JOHN: "The subject is closed. Don't bring it up again."

DONNA MARIE: "But it is past time for me to retire."

JOHN: "I am tired of talking about it. You are not selling this house!"

How could he be so reckless with my retirement money?

My head spun. None of this made sense. Why would he put our seventeen-year relationship on the line for a house? There would be other houses, but what I thought was important was our relationship. How could the person that I loved so much act this way? How could the person who "loved me so much" carry on this way about my house? How could he be so reckless with my retirement money? It took me many years and a lot of overtime, working nights and weekends with extensive travel, to get to the point where I was financially ready to retire. The irony did not escape me that I was living in an old one-bedroom apartment, preparing to retire, while he was living like a king in my four-bedroom house with a pool in a country club community, blocking my retirement. Did he really expect me to provide him with a free house? Where on earth would he get an idea like that? During this time of extreme turbulence and turmoil in our relationship was when my mother died. I felt like I was being crushed from two sides.

4. The Threats Begin

One month later, while in Arizona on vacation, he brought up the subject of the house.

JOHN: "The realtor said the house is worth $725,000!"

DONNA MARIE: "Great, it is time to sell it."

JOHN: "What? Sell it? I thought you'd be happy about the house."

DONNA MARIE: "I am very happy. I am thrilled. It's time to sell it."

The First Threat

Then he threatened me. As it turns out, this was the first of several to come. But this one was the big one; it was the first threat. It broke new ground in our relationship and changed the rules. It set the new pattern for his behavior and a new low in our now troubled and deteriorating relationship.

...it was the first threat. It broke new ground in our relationship and changed the rules.

After my mother died, I guess that without the constant stress and strain of her failing health and the time required to organize her care in five different facilities over the prior year, I was just beginning to turn my attention back to my retirements plans—now six months past due. I believe that as I ramped up the intensity, so did he. And he played the masterful victim. Of course, he was the aggressor, but he considered himself the victim. After all, in his mind, somehow he deserved a free house from me. Why? I have no idea.

...he was the aggressor, but he considered himself the victim.

For years prior we had long agreed that we would each contribute an equal amount of capital to a joint household fund for us to live on and that our other funds would remain separate. So I was quite puzzled by these new developments that were not a 50/50 split.

JOHN: "This is not what I expected. I thought you would be happy about the value of the house."

DONNA MARIE: "I will be happy when I sell that house and I am able to retire. Take the money and run."

JOHN: "You are ruining my vacation. I don't want to hear any more about selling that house."

DONNA MARIE: "But I need the money from the house for *my* retirement."

JOHN: "No, you don't."

DONNA MARIE: "Yes, I do. I never planned to have such a huge amount of capital tied up in a house for my retirement. I need to sell it to get my money out. I will live on that money."

JOHN: "I am really upset about this. It is a great house. You will learn to like it. You can play tennis somewhere else."

DONNA MARIE: "I do like the house alright; it's just way too expensive."

JOHN: "If you even think about selling that house, I can't tell you what I am going to do."

DONNA MARIE: "What is that supposed to mean?"

JOHN:	"The subject is closed. Now don't ruin my vacation."
DONNA MARIE:	"What?"
JOHN:	"The subject is closed. Don't you bring it up again."

Under normal circumstances, I would have told him to take a flying leap. But these were not normal times. I was still reeling from the following:

But these were not normal times. I was still reeling…

- my mother's medical error
- her one-year treatment ordeal
- all the conflicting medical opinions
- her ups and downs with hope and no hope
- her falling and failing
- callous treatment from some of the doctors
- pleading for my brothers to visit my mother
- complex and emotional end-of-life decisions
- my mother's eventual death
- handling her affairs and estate.

I was completely exhausted and totally tapped out emotionally and physically.

Needless to say, I had a few things on my mind, and I was completely exhausted and totally tapped out emotionally and physically. The one person that I counted on to be my life partner, my best friend, my soul mate, the one to help me through life's crises had turned into a selfish, aggressive bully.

He high-jacked my house; he blocked my retirement. I was an emotional wreck. In no way was I prepared to lose my mother and my almost eighteen-year relationship with John within a single month. It was too much to think about and too much to bear.

It was too much to think about and too much to bear.

Given my severely weakened state and my deep feelings of loss, his first threat worked very well. He had a front-row seat through it all. He had helped me enormously in dealing with arrangements for my mother over the past three years or so. But he knew weakness when he saw it, and I guess he was determined to use it to his full advantage.

Now my thoughts churned and spun. Theoretically, we were vacationing in lovely Sedona—in one of my favorite loved places with my favorite person on earth. But I was really in hell. Now my alleged soul mate cared more about my house than he cared about me. He wanted to marry my house!

How could this have happened? I thought, *I am smart and successful. I am ready to retire comfortably with my man. How did this all go so terribly wrong? How can someone possibly expect—no wait, demand—a free house?*

None of this made any sense to me. We had always shared and split everything; we decided from the very beginning that we could go out a lot more if we divided everything, which we did almost 50/50. Occasionally, for example, when we were out with his kids, he would pay for me. Other times, we'd have a real date, and he would pay. But most of the time, we split all our expenses evenly. He was perpetually digging out from under his extensive family and business obligations. Our arrangement to split everything worked out just fine, and we went out all of the time.

...our relationship was on the line with my house—unbelievable. But now our relationship was on the line with my house—unbelievable. Head over heels in love with him, my world revolved around him. I planned to spend the rest of my life with him. Other than my job, he *was* my life. My mother's protracted illness and death had taken a huge toll on me. But now, my retirement was in jeopardy. Even my retirement date had come and gone. I curled up in a ball. I could not explain what was happening in my life. *Other than my job, he was my life.*

How could a man (at times, so caring, dependable, reasonable, and fair) now be acting this way? He had helped me so much with my mother. How could he possibly do this to me? To tell you the truth, I still don't fully understand it. But in the context of controlling behavior, it now makes a little more sense. I was trying to move him out of my house where he had become extremely comfortable. Who wouldn't be comfortable paying $2,000 a month for a $725,000 house? I guess he viewed it as a threat to his lifestyle; so to him, this was war. Sadly, I did not realize it at the time.

CHAPTER 6

My Physical Setback

"If you don't have your health, you don't have anything."
— Anonymous

1. The Painful Pinched Nerve

One month after the first threat in Arizona and two months after my mother's death, I suffered a very painful injury—a pinched nerve in my neck. There is no way of knowing for sure whether it was related to the immense stress from the combination of my mother's illness and of John's selfish and belligerent interference in my retirement finances. Half of the people tell me: Absolutely yes, it was definitely related. Others say: No, the injury occurred solely because you had been leaning over a computer eleven hours a day for decades.

It all began after working a long day on the Friday before Memorial Day in 2006. I started work that morning as I typically did around 7:30 a.m. John planned to meet me downtown at 7:00 p.m. that evening to go to the theater, so I worked straight through as usual.

But just before 7:00 p.m., my right shoulder started to scream in pain. I took some Motrin and hoped for the best. But it continued to grow worse by the hour. By Sunday morning, my right hand and arm were quite swollen. If I hadn't removed my ring from my right hand, the ring would've needed to be cut off. John took me to an urgent care clinic where an X-ray of my neck indicated that nothing was broken but that an MRI would be required. I was prescribed some pain pills, thankfully, to take the edge off the pain.

Pins and needles shot down my right arm and hand without any reprieve.

Because of this injury, I could not use my right hand. Pains shot across my shoulder and down my arm. My right forearm hardened into a knot. Pins and needles shot down my right arm and hand without any reprieve. I found it hard to sleep and difficult to stay asleep. I had to lie on my back or left side to get any rest—a very fitful rest at that.

On the Tuesday after Memorial Day, I dropped into my doctor's office at 8 a.m. without an appointment and pleaded for a prescription for an MRI. A couple of days later, I had the MRI, but it took two weeks to see a neurologist to interpret the results. In the meantime, I forced myself to work half days even though I was in intense pain. And I was worried.

I was barely surviving. I mustered all of my energy to work 4.5 hours per day. Then I would go home and go straight to bed to get ready to do it all over again the next day. It was very scary. And it was quite humbling. There I was—a tennis player, an athlete of sorts—who could barely move. I barely functioned. A sympathetic work colleague suggested that I try acupuncture while I waited for the neurologist. At that point, I was willing to try anything. I found the acupuncture to be very soothing, but I can't honestly say that it relieved my pain.

After two weeks elapsed, I got in to see the neurologist. The MRI showed bone spurs in two cervical joints. The neurologist said that no surgery was needed. I was very relieved to hear that news: I had always heard horror stories about neck and back surgery. Maybe my injury was not so bad after all. The neurologist authorized me to work half days for a month and set me up for a course of physical therapy (PT).

I had to wait two weeks to get a PT appointment so I continued with the acupuncture. I was not sure if it helped, but at least I was doing something. And it was very soothing and relaxing, which couldn't be all bad given the year that I had had so far. When I started going to PT, they began traction treatments. As it turns out, I loved traction. I bet you thought you would never hear anyone say that—but I loved traction and still do.

I loved traction. I bet you thought you would never hear anyone say that…

There is very little space in your neck and spine for nerves, bones, and discs. It is actually a real estate issue; everything must stay in its place or else there is trouble. I had inflammation and bone spurs on my neck that encroached into the nerve space—thus the pain. Traction pulled everything apart so there was room for all of the pieces to go where they belonged. And then there was no pain.

However, problematically, I returned to work directly after PT. The PT session expanded the space in my spine and relieved my pain. Going back to my work on the computer compressed my spine again and brought back the pain. In one hour at work, I undid all of the benefits of the PT. I needed to go to PT after work so that the benefits endured well beyond the actual session. I would need to keep working short days. I began a limited exercise regime, but it was still too early to see whether it helped.

I called my neurologist to secure another note to authorize me to continue to work half days. But he was on vacation. As it turns out, no one was covering for him. The nurse said that there were no instructions otherwise and that I would just have to start working full days—too bad. Thank you so much for your overwhelming compassion!

Looking back, perhaps because I was not a candidate for surgery, I fell off the radar at the neurologist's office. Apparently, I was out of sight, out of mind. I called him a neurologist, but he called himself a neurosurgeon. Therein lies the difference.

I called him a neurologist, but he called himself a neurosurgeon. Therein lies the difference.

2. The Medical Runaround—Take Two

I begged to see another neurologist. I was still in extreme pain, and I needed to continue to work half days. They cited over and over that it was not their policy to have one neurologist cover for another. It didn't make any sense to me. They said I would just have to go back to working full time. The nurse would not give me a note for work, and she was not going to bother the doctor on his vacation for a non-emergency.

I begged and pleaded. They finally relented and gave me another doctor to see. As long as I was seeing someone, it was fine with me. The new doctor gave me the half-day work authorization and prescribed more pain pills and more PT visits. But I was still in a lot of pain. Working on the computer undid much of the progress from PT, so I was stuck in a loop. The exercises started to work—just a little, but the situation looked very bleak. I merely existed. I put forth a huge effort to work 4.5 hours a day and then went straight home to bed.

...it looked like I had met my match. At this point, I was afraid that I would never, ever, get any better. I still had pins all the time as well as periodic sharp pains. It was indeed a sad time in my life. I had always overcome obstacles and blasted through limitations. In this instance, though, it looked like I had met my match.

It was time to do some serious thinking. I could end up disabled; I might never get better. Maybe, it would be best if John moved on. *Yes, he should go*, I thought. I asked my fiancé to leave me behind. He did not sign up to marry an invalid. It's one thing if your spouse gets sick. But before you're married, you can opt out.

DONNA MARIE: "Just go—it's OK. I will not think less of you if you leave now."

JOHN: "That is crazy talk."

DONNA MARIE: "I am damaged goods. Just go. Please go."

JOHN: "I am staying."

...in my physical, mental, and emotional condition, I did not have the energy to forcibly evict him. Looking back, I just really wanted him out of my house. I wanted to sell it, but he refused to leave. What kind of man would he be if he left me now? Sure, he was still in control of my house; he wasn't going anywhere. And, in my physical, mental, and emotional condition, I did not have the energy to forcibly evict him.

I was so upset. If I could have simply retired when I planned, then none of this would have happened to me. I had already worked nine months longer than I had intended. And now, I was injured to boot. I couldn't believe all of my current trials. But I felt powerless to act given the severity of the injury and the depths of my emotional pain.

I went back to see the second neurologist, and he was certain that I had carpal tunnel syndrome in my right wrist. He was still somewhat perturbed that I was another doctor's patient. I did not know why at the time, so I just ignored his displeasure. He ran a series of tests on me in a physical examination, and what do you know, I did *not* have carpal tunnel syndrome after all. Now he did not know what I had, so he ordered an EMG test.

I cannot begin to describe how painful an EMG test is if you already have severe nerve pain from just sitting still. To conduct it, they stuck two-inch needles into the nerves in my right arm, which were already screaming. Then they turned on the juice and shocked the nerves ten times to gauge the reaction. Ouch! Ouch! Ouch! was the reaction. I was in excruciating pain during the test. I sure hoped that the test meant that I was on a path to get better when it showed the doctor what really was going on.

When the EMG report came in, I was so excited that a remedy was truly in my future. *I am going to get better*, I thought, *just wait and see!* The second neurologist announced triumphantly that he now knew what was wrong with me. Drum roll, please!

> Dr: "You have a pinched nerve in your neck."
>
> DONNA MARIE: "We already knew that—I came in with that diagnosis."   *"Yes, but now I know it."*
>
> Dr.:   "Yes, but now *I* know it."

So all of this time, he thought that I was faking it, shopping for pain pills, and trying to dodge work. Did I look like a drug abuser? Did I look like a bum? I was used to working fifty-hour weeks for goodness sake. Did he think I was a liar, that my pain was fake?

When I composed myself enough for polite discourse, he remarked that there was no way for doctors to know for certain who was faking their pain, and yes, it was a huge industry. Think of the ubiquitous slip-and-fall scams

***Please don't dare
call this health CARE.*** and you will begin to get the picture. Maybe so, but thanks a lot for your vote of confidence in me, doctor! Please don't dare call this health *CARE*.

After the doctor finally believed that my pain was real, he ordered more PT sessions plus a series of three cortisone shots for my spine. He transferred my care coordination over to a pain specialist to manage my treatments in the future. Maybe this was the answer that I had been hoping for; I went forward with a little hope and my fingers crossed.

3. The Medical Dream Team

Once again, I prepared to get better. Even with major pain, constant pins and needles in my right arm and hand, and working part time, now there was a ray of hope. I still worked in pain, but the PT exercises started to work. Yes, those awkward shoulder squeezes and silly head turns were the answer to my prayers. And Mark Lee, the physical therapist, was a very skilled and patient practitioner. Now, maybe the series of cortisone injections was just the ticket to a full recovery. *Oh, could it be?* I hoped. *Is there a light at the end of the tunnel? Will I soon return to my amateur athlete status?*

I scheduled the first cortisone shot in my spine with great anticipation, and I must say a little fear as well. I would never dare to have a needle inserted into my spine unless there were extreme circumstances. But if the cortisone would decrease the inflammation, perhaps my recovery could be accelerated. Yes, I would try anything that might relieve the pain and get me back on track. My fingers, on my left hand, were crossed during the procedure. I hoped for the best. I visualized myself playing tennis again, serving, volleying, and celebrating a victory.

The first cortisone injection truly made me feel better. It reduced the pressure on my spine and neck, which then decreased my pain. As a result, I slept better and work became easier over time. I gradually started to expand my work day in half-hour increments; now, I was up to 5.5 hour days. I cut way back on the pain pills. I finished my prescribed PT sessions and did the exercises on my own. I also had a home traction machine that I used twice a week to replace the treatments by the physical therapist.

The doctor suggested that I schedule the second cortisone injection in about a month. Unlike my neurologist friends, this pain specialist was truly a compassionate soul. He was very attentive, he listened, and he seemed to care. He gave me what I needed. Because the first injection really made me feel better, I had faith in this doctor so I signed up for the second one.

That turned out to be a big mistake. Sometimes it is better to leave well enough alone. The second injection made me feel much worse. In fact, it took me all the way back to the beginning of my recovery. The doctor explained that this sometimes happens.

Sometimes it is better to leave well enough alone.

Here we go again, I worried. When my favorite therapist saw my name back in the appointment book after I had "graduated from PT," he wondered, "Now what?" More pain, more pins, more PT, more pain pills. *Back to the starting line*, I thought direly, *oh my goodness*. But then I rallied; I did it once—I could do it again.

When it was all said and done, it took me ten months to reach recovery where I could type for myself and work a full day. All told, it involved 544 hours of sick leave, 40 physical therapy appointments, 2 cortisone injections in my spine, and 8 occupational therapy appointments to strengthen my right hand.

But I recovered. Hooray!

CHAPTER 7

Real Estate Collapse Begins

"What goes up must come down."
– Anonymous

1. Decision Time: I Give Up

Seven months after the onset of my pinched nerve, as the snowbird season approached in December 2006, I was now ready to forcibly evict John. If the sheriff had to come and pile his furniture out on the curb, then so be it. It was long past time. I had conquered a severe injury, which gifted me with plenty of time to think. My fiancé was not acting like my life partner, my soul mate, the love of my life. Something had changed in him, and it altered everything. He behaved so selfishly and belligerently that I no longer was willing to go to ridiculous lengths to save our "so-called" relationship.

If the sheriff had to come and pile his furniture out on the curb, then so be it.

I kept striving to save a relationship that was not worth saving after all.

I was trying to keep us together. I attempted everything that I knew to do this with care. But only one of us acted like a loving fiancée; so I gave up. I considered the relationship over because I was working on it alone. It was hopeless; I kept striving to save a relationship that was not worth saving after all.

He'd lost his power over me; the spell had been broken. But unfortunately, that was only the beginning of the story.

55

I called the realtor to list the house. He said that the market had softened significantly and that I should have sold the house the year before. *No kidding!* I thought. He said he did not know how to price it because there was not much activity but suggested $725,000 to start as an exploratory price just to gauge the market reaction, then we would adjust it as needed.

$725,000? The same price as eight months before? Amazed, I wondered if maybe I dodged a bullet here. Maybe all of the interference and the foot dragging when my mother was dying and I was suffering with a pinched nerve had not hurt me in the real estate market after all. *Oh, could it be?* I hoped.

Maybe there was universal justice. Yes, my fiancé had highjacked my house, but maybe I would still be able to sell it and move on. I could retire and start a new life without him. Maybe I could still get out of this mess in one piece. Maybe it would all work out after all.

> *Maybe there was universal justice.*

2. The Market Is Unimpressed

Maybe not. The market reaction was a complete yawn.

The price of $725,000 lasted for three weeks without a peep, so we lowered it to $699,000. That price lasted for two weeks without any activity although full-on snowbird season usually brings a bustle of real estate activity. We lowered the price again to $665,000, which lasted for three weeks, and then we lowered it to $635,000. Okay, with that $90,000 price drop in two months—I was getting very worried.

At the new listing price of $635,000, my fiancé became enraged, even livid. He thought that I was crazy and that I was just giving the house away. So I immediately took the house off the market.

> *He thought that I was crazy and that I was just giving the house away.*

Because he thought the price was so low, I asked him to buy half of the house; I agreed to stay in the house for a few years. The gains that I was trying to capture were gone. At a $635,000 list price, I would likely net a maximum of $550,000 under the most ideal conditions, and these were anything but ideal conditions! Even though there were no tennis facilities, I knew that I could make it work. It obviously was not my first choice, but things were what they were. I had missed the market, and I accepted that. My placeholder had done its work beautifully, but my fiancé had interfered in the planned sale. So in order to save the relationship and stop the incessant arguing, we would stay for a while and then re-evaluate our options later after he sold his business.

But wait! After all of that and his outrage at the ridiculously low $635,000 listing price, he adamantly refused to buy half. Let me get this straight: He vehemently demanded that I keep the house when it was worth $725,000. Now that I agreed to stay, the house was listed at $635,000, and he thought that I was giving it away, but he obstinately refused to buy half. I could only conclude that he expected me to provide him with a free house. *What?* I questioned in my head. *Who gets a free house?*

This was just nuts. I put the house back on the market the same week. The realtors just shook their heads, but they had no idea what was going on with us. Everyone on the outside saw him as a charming, gracious, generous, intelligent, and caring man; so had I for sixteen years! He was one of the most popular members of the golf club.

Everyone on the outside saw him as a charming, gracious, generous, intelligent, and caring man...

Believe me, you have no idea what may be going on in someone else's relationship. You have no idea how the private persona differs from the public one, which is just what these controlling types count on.

Something in my fiancé snapped, and he entered what I call the "overt control" phase; he was no longer my soul mate. After he moved into my house, he changed dramatically. And no one else saw the side of him that I saw.

Three weeks later, I almost had a buyer. A couple spent more than six hours in the house. It was so close. They kept coming back and looking and looking. But it was not meant to be—no offer, no sale.

John instructed the poor realtors to take the lock box off every time he had company and put it back on when his company left. Apparently, he had lied to his family, telling them that he owned the house, so he could not possibly explain why it would be on the market. Everyone knew how much he loved that house. But it only became clear to me how much more he loved my house than he loved me; I guess I was a little slow. And I believe that he just hoped that I would give up and not sell the house after all and marry him, leaving his lie undetected.

3. House Prices in Free Fall

By now, the other realtors became very aggressive with the listing prices, sensing the panic in the air. The last one out of Florida, please turn off the lights. Many people just wanted to sell and move

The last one out of Florida, please turn off the lights.

on; but alas, there were no buyers. One realtor who showed my house said that it was *way* overpriced. *Oh dear, how much lower can it go?*

I listed with a new realtor. This time the starting price was $599,000. I wanted to be aggressive so that the property finally sold. I wanted this to be over. I had learned my lesson: No one should have the right or ability to mess with my money and my retirement. I had believed in and trusted the wrong man. I was so sorry. But this new price lasted for four weeks with no interest. The new lower price was $550,000, but still not a peep.

I thank God that I did not quit my job. That was my financial lifeline. But no matter how much money I could earn, I could not earn it as fast as my house lost it. The house value dropped $50,000 in one month! I kept running my monthly net worth statement, and things grew increasingly bleak. Each month was much worse than the month before.

I thank God that I did not quit my job. That was my financial lifeline.

CHAPTER 8

The Relationship Unravels

"No legacy is so rich as honesty."
– William Shakespeare

1. The Second Threat

As the price of "his" beloved house kept falling, John grew more livid, cynical, and mean. The stage was now set. I guess that after the first threat worked and he succeeded in delaying my decision to put the house on the market, he thought he would give it another try.

JOHN: "I see that you lowered the price, again. Don't you dare give this house away!"

DONNA MARIE: "Will you buy half?"

JOHN: "No! But I am going to be very upset with you if you give this house away. This is a great house."

DONNA MARIE: "Will you buy half?"

JOHN: "No! But our relationship might not make it if you give it away."

DONNA MARIE: "Will you buy half?"

JOHN: "No! Drop it already."

DONNA MARIE:	"Then it shouldn't matter to you what price I get for my house. It is my retirement money. You didn't lose anything."
JOHN:	"Yes, I did. I bought the furniture."
DONNA MARIE:	"I offered to buy the furniture last year, but you got so angry at the idea. You heatedly said, 'You're not taking the furniture!'"
JOHN:	"I don't remember that."
DONNA MARIE:	"There is no point discussing this if you are going to rewrite history."

The second and subsequent threats had no impact on me. I had already done all that I could do by putting the house on the market and by repeatedly lowering the price based on deteriorating market conditions. But his situational amnesia was incredibly frustrating. There was no way to have a productive conversation with him. If a topic was in any way uncomfortable for him, he simply would not remember it—very convenient indeed. I had to just stand there and watch my money, retirement plans, and my long-term relationship slowly descend in a death spiral.

Please let me get out of this nightmare.

Please, please, please! Someone please buy my house so that this chapter of my life can come to an end. I learned my lesson. I'm sorry. Please let me get out of this nightmare.

Please!

2. Offer of Reconciliation

In an amazing turn of events, out of the blue, John—the man suffering from severe situational amnesia—acknowledged what he had done and recognized how seriously my life and finances had been affected by his actions. This was truly unbelievable. I had completely given up hope on him.

By now, I had been with this man for nineteen years. Before this horrible house incident, I had trusted him very much. We had so much in common and largely held to the same beliefs and opinions. We even liked to

Could it really be true that this relationship was salvageable after all of this carnage?

do the same things. So perhaps my faith in him was not misplaced after all. Could it really be true that this relationship was salvageable after all of this carnage?

When he admitted his role in the house fiasco, it obviously had important financial implications. He did realize this. So John put an offer on the table to pay most of my living expenses until I turned 62 when I would be eligible to collect social security and a small pension from one of my employers.

It was an amazing offer, especially given the events of the past year. Maybe we could work this out after all. No, let's rephrase that: I was sure that we could work this out now given this new turn of events. We were both reasonable people; we were both in business. We could do this. We were meant to be together. Hope springs eternal.

Things were indeed looking up. From the darkest days, now there arose a ray of hope. The relationship would be saved. I knew it. I knew it all along. We'd be just fine now. I had bet my future on him, and now my bet was about to pay off. Happily ever after here I come. See! My life partner would not fail me.

From the darkest days, now there arose a ray of hope. The relationship would be saved.

He wanted me to quit working so that we could begin our life together. But I couldn't quit my job as long as so much of my retirement money was tied up in the house. We started working on a spreadsheet that had eight years across the top and approximately forty expense categories down the left. We agreed that he would pay the rent, utilities, maintenance and repairs, all food eaten in, gas and oil changes for both cars, health and first aid supplies, household items, and other items too numerous to list here. I factored in inflation and contingencies so that the budget would be as realistic as possible to make sure that it would really work on his income alone.

We agreed that I would pay my car insurance and car repairs, my health insurance, my long-term care insurance, beauty supplies, and other items too numerous to list here and that we would continue to split expenses for eating out, entertainment out, and vacations. I ran the numbers with modest inflation estimates. He was confident that he could swing the costs. After all, he was still garnering a full salary from his business without working and still had no plans to sell his business.

...we would be splitting the expected losses from the house. I was amazed. The present value of his contribution going out eight years accounted for almost fifty percent of my projected loss. This was truly a fair offer. In effect, we would be splitting the expected losses from the house. It should have never happened in the first place. He had no right to interfere in my selling the house, especially when my mother was so near death and he could plainly see that I was under extreme duress. But at this point, covering fifty percent of my losses sounded like a viable offer. And it would save our relationship. Yes, this was a good offer. All was well again. I accepted and was very relieved. My faith in him was restored.

My faith in him was restored.

Up to this point, I had been questioning everything. As a professional ruminator, I went over and over the facts in my mind. Perhaps because we were long-term companions, there was no fire in our relationship. Yes, I had been focused largely on my career. Yes, he had concentrated on digging out from his extensive family obligations. But along the way, there was truly an "us." Yes, it had been unconventional, but I always chalked that up to our circumstances being unconventional.

But perhaps there was nothing deeper between us after all. Were we just good buddies after all of this time together? All I know is that I loved him very much; he was at the very core of my life. I always believed that he was there standing beside me; he was my rock. When the rest of the world gave me grief, he gave me comfort, up until the house fiasco, that is. I could not attempt to describe his feelings for me or the role that I played in his life. But all I know is that he was the most important person in my life and that I very much looked forward to spending the rest of my life with him.

We were back on our way. I knew we could work things out like level-headed adults. I just knew it. After a major setback and on the brink of a total wipe out, we were back on track—this time for good! Things would be great. All of our plans would turn into reality. We would travel, have fun, and go dancing. After I stopped working, we would have so much more time to be together. We were soul mates. Yes, we would be very close. We would enjoy each other's company. This was indeed the beginning of the really good times.

After a major setback and on the brink of a total wipe out, we were back on track…

Both of us had worked very hard, and now we had finally arrived, together.

After working more than fifty hours a week, late nights, weekends, and traveling extensively for decades, it was finally *my* time. And he had paid all of his enormous family commitments. So it was now *our* time—at last. Both of us had worked very hard, and now we had finally arrived, together.

I was so glad that I had not forcibly evicted him to free up my capital when it was time for me to retire. It was not in my character or in my values; I always believed that we could work things out. Reconciliation was at all times very important to me.

But this series of events cost me dearly; I still worked full time two years after my planned retirement date. But now, he had stepped in to save the day. I didn't know what happened in all of this, but my faith in him had been restored.

I started to calculate a new retirement date. I would be paid for all of my unused vacation days so, whenever possible, it was best to move the payments into a new tax year. Consequently, January was usually the best month to retire, and I wanted to work on the date carefully. There was also a slim chance that I could qualify for a buyout from my employer. They often had programs where they try to usher out senior staff to make room for younger, lower-paid staff. So I attempted to work out a buyout proposal that would be accepted. I was getting back on track financially. Happy days were here again!

3. Not So Fast

"The devil's most devilish when respectable."
– Elizabeth Barrett Browning

At least for a few weeks anyway.

I started firming up my planning dates and possible buyout options. But it was all for naught. Almost as quickly as we developed the spreadsheet, cracks began to form in the foundation.

Out of the blue once again, he had a few other ideas. He backed out of our deal. Under the new plan, he decided that he would *not* pay my living expenses until I was 62 as we agreed. He determined, on his own, that I should contribute $2,000 a month toward my living expenses and that he would then pay the rest.

I own the house and I am to pay $2,000 a month? What? If I am paying $2,000 a month, then why do I need him? What help is that? What happened to acknowledging that his vehement demands played the major role in causing this mess in the first place?

This was a total disaster. After I had completely lost confidence in him and we had hit bottom, he restored my faith in him by accepting full responsibility for his actions. He offered to pay my living expenses until I was 62. Except now, he was backing out of our deal. This was bad—very bad. Now, I did not trust him. I couldn't believe a word that he said; there was Dr. Jekyll and Mr. Hyde right there in front of me. I needed to escape once and for all.

4. The Third Threat Issued

I guess it was only predictable that he would threaten me again. I was still a captive until that house sold. It looked like, unless I planned to lose even more money, I was trapped with him as my tenant until the sale of the home.

Perhaps he sensed my situation. So why not another threat? I understand that once someone starts to threaten people there is usually no good reason to stop. In fact, they tend to escalate the threats. The third threat was that I must quit working by December 2008; he wanted his companion there in Florida with him. The dialogue went something like this:

> JOHN: "You said you were going to quit working in 2005. What happened?"

> DONNA MARIE: "You picked my house instead of me."

> JOHN: "No, that wasn't it. You just wanted to keep on working."

> DONNA MARIE: "Really, I needed to sell my house to get my retirement money out."

> JOHN: "Well, time is a wasting. I am not getting any younger. You need to retire by December 2008. I am not going to wait for you any longer than that."

> DONNA MARIE: "Is that a threat?"

> JOHN: "No, I am just saying…."

> DONNA MARIE: "Well, it sounds like a threat to me."

> JOHN: "Well, you have messed up our retirement plans because you are still working. You will never stop working."

> DONNA MARIE: "I lost a lot of money on the house. I need to keep working."

> JOHN: "That's not the reason."

> DONNA MARIE: "Sure, you throw away a ton of my money, and I'm supposed to quit working. That doesn't make sense to me."

> JOHN: "Never mind."

Pressure and lies, lies, and more lies. I didn't even expect him to tell the truth anymore. I had given up. Please, please let this be over. The sooner the better!

5. The Third Threat Withdrawn

Almost as soon as the third threat arrived on the scene, he rescinded it.

JOHN: "I realized that when I said that you needed to quit working by December 2008 that I was coming on a little strong."

DONNA MARIE: "That's certainly what I thought. So what are you saying now?"

JOHN: "I am saying that I think that it is best for you to decide for yourself when you want to quit working. Otherwise, you will be a nervous wreck and not very happy."

DONNA MARIE: "Well, thank you very much for your consideration. That makes me feel somewhat better."

The situation was very troubling. John never used to threaten me; he was always very polite, a gentleman. He opened my car door for me. Yet lately, he seemed to be threatening me about everything. Maybe now that he had rescinded this threat, he would stop bullying me for good. The threats only damaged what was left of our relationship. Cautiously optimistic, a quiet peace settled over the land. But alas, the peace was short lived.

CHAPTER 9

The Real Estate Collapse Deepens

"…Monetary policy contributed very little to the recent housing bubble in the U.S."
– Ben Bernanke

1. The Price Keeps Falling

Florida was the new wasteland for real estate. It was no longer "real" estate at all but rather "surreal" estate. This house—and this man—destroyed my dreams. And the price kept falling.

$509,000

$475,000

$450,000

Please, would someone, anyone out there, please buy this stupid house at any *price?*

2. The Price Falls Some More

"The shifts of fortune test the reliability of friends."
– Marcus Tullius Cicero

When the house finally fell below what I paid for it five years earlier, John started to drool. He said that he wanted to buy it for himself. He truly loved that house; it was his pride and joy, the center of his life. Perhaps it filled out his identity. He was so happy in a new house with new furniture for the first time in his life. I guess the house became his emblem of success. After years and years of extensive family and business obligations, he had arrived. Perhaps the house signified his accomplishment; the only problem was that it was my house.

> *I guess the house became his emblem of success. After years and years of extensive family and business obligations, he had arrived.*

I asked him to go ahead and make me an offer so that the house that he loved more than anything in the world would be all his. He would then own and control the most valuable thing in his life—his dream house—forever.

But in a perverse twist, he decided that he would not make an offer on the house until I received another offer; he did not want to overpay for it. What? Because there were no buyers, by definition there was no market, and thus no fair market value. He wanted to wait to claim his prize at a killer price, not caring how much money I lost. Looking out for number one was his game plan.

Is my fiancé really truly just a selfish and vindictive controller who is now out to punish me? I wondered sadly. He later denied that this incident ever happened, but I have e-mails that said he would offer me less for the house because I reduced the price. He never did present an offer for his dream house—what an incredible missed opportunity for him to secure true happiness.

3. The Physical Toll on Me

As I watched my net worth, my relationship, and my retirement plans go down the drain, I began to experience panic attacks in the middle of the night. I would bolt straight up in bed gasping for air with my heart pounding out of my chest. It was truly frightening. Each night I thought I was going to die. It took approximately twenty minutes to settle my heart

> *Each night I thought I was going to die.*

rate down to a manageable level and then about two hours to get back to sleep. It was scary and exhausting.

A deep feeling of sadness and despair had set in. *How low can the house go? When will this end?* There was no way of knowing.

As soon as I left work and got in my car, I would start crying uncontrollably. I sobbed all the way home, every day. This went on for weeks. I had nowhere to go and nobody to turn to. My best friend had turned into my worst enemy— at the worst possible time of my life. I was unprepared for this mentally, emotionally, physically, or financially.

How can he possibly treat me like this after all that we meant to each other? After all we've been through? After all of the talk about our bright and loving future together? It was a time of true despair. And it was about to get worse before it got better.

4. Finally, the Sale

The new price was set at $425,000, which was now well below what I paid for the house. Surely, this new price would be low enough to attract a buyer or even multiple buyers. Sure enough, there was a flurry of activity with dozens of people coming to see the house. I crossed my fingers, hoping that my nightmare would finally be over once and for all.

However, only one person was interested in my house, and she could not afford it. Instead she was going to buy a smaller villa. My realtor worked out the arrangements, and she made me an offer on my house at the price of the villa. After her offer was in, my realtor canvassed the other realtors who had showed the house to see if there were any other potential offers being considered. Even with the flurry of activity and the excellent pricing, sadly, there were none.

I sold the house to the lady for $370,000. As a reminder, the listing began at $725,000, and the house sold for $370,000. The sale that could have netted me $650,000 in 2005 instead netted me $340,000 in 2008. Thanks to my fiancé for high-jacking my house when my mother's health drastically faded and for sabotaging my retirement! But it all worked out for him; he got out with barely a scratch.

With my fiancé's interference, I lost $310,000 in capital plus another $60,000 in interest for the 2.5 years I was unable to use the $650,000 capital. What a guy! I needlessly flushed $370,000 down the drain because of him. Simply incredible. Needless to say, I never envisioned our partnership working out this way.

...I never envisioned our partnership working out this way.

My fiancé found a rental house and moved about twenty-five doors down the street; all of his furniture fit in just fine. That was my plan a long time before, but there was no point in rehashing it now that the damage had all been done—to me. All of my money was already water under the bridge—up in smoke, whatever. Gone!

After the sale and the move, I walked on eggshells. I successfully removed him from my house. I wrapped, packed, and boxed to make sure he was out on time. I was very worried that he would find some way to jeopardize the closing or leave a mess behind, but thankfully, he did not. *Thank you for that small concession as a human being, John,* I thought. But I didn't trust him at all.

CHAPTER 10

The Relationship Unravels Further

"Nobody who ever gave his best regretted it."
– George Halas

1. Mediation, or Not

After my fiancé settled comfortably into his new place, I asked the first realtor for the name of a real estate mediator who specialized in related-party transactions. I offered my fiancé the choice between two names. He was very surprised that I wanted to pursue external advice. The dialogue went something like this:

DONNA MARIE: "I'd like to sort this mess out with mediation. Here are two names; you pick the one you'd prefer to see."

JOHN: "What? There is nothing to sort out."

DONNA MARIE: "You interfered in the sale of my house, and because of that, I lost a fortune."

JOHN: "I am not talking about this with anyone."

DONNA MARIE: "You interfered in the sale of my house."

JOHN: "Let it go."

DONNA MARIE: "Easy for you to say!"

He refused to go to a mediator or even to talk about it. He was angry. After all, the house was my problem and my loss—not his.

2. The Fourth Threat

"Although people who indulge in oppressive behaviors may apologize in order to avoid the consequences of their hurtful actions...rarely can they cry for the other."
– Patricia Evans

It wasn't long after his move that our "relationship" began to crumble even more rapidly. No longer my tenant, I did not have to worry anymore about John damaging my property in a spite-fest. I could no longer pretend that we had a relationship or that we were still engaged. We floated through on autopilot going through the motions of a relationship. I grew even more distant after the housing crisis was behind me. On a Saturday evening in Florida, he said:

> JOHN: "You are not very affectionate anymore. You never hug me now. You never greet me anymore. I just want things to be the way they used to be—before the house."
>
> DONNA MARIE: "This relationship has very serious problems."
>
> JOHN: "Then maybe we should split."
>
> DONNA MARIE: "Okay."

I stayed up all night and packed my things in John's new rental home. Boxes, boxes, boxes! Over the past four years, I had moved a lot of stuff to Florida gradually in suitcases when I visited every other weekend. How ironic that now I was packing it all to be moved back up north. Oh, well.

While I packed, I encountered a significant problem: Because the next day was Sunday, none of the approximately twenty storage places would be open. The next day, when I started making calls at various storage facilities, I finally found one where someone answered the phone. Yes, they were open on Sunday—victory at last! I asked John for one last favor and requested that he drive me and my boxes to the storage place and then to the airport. After that, I would be out of his life forever. He said that was not what he wanted at all, but he would drive me. He tested me once to assess my resolve to leave, but it was a fake out.

With just three hours to get my stuff out of his place and into storage, I finished packing. After all of this nonsense, I was ready to go. I would not curl up in a ball and die without him after all. He sabotaged my retirement and destroyed our relationship; he shattered any future we might have had together.

He kindly loaded my boxes into his car. We drove down the road, out of the community, on to the local roads, and then on to the interstate. Halfway to the storage facility, he turned to me and spoke.

JOHN:	"What did you want me to say?"
DONNA MARIE:	"I want you to acknowledge your role in my massive financial loss on the house, and I want you to apologize to me."
JOHN:	"Okay, I acknowledge my role in the house loss, and I do apologize."
DONNA MARIE:	"Okay, then. Turn the car around and go back to your place. Because you acknowledged your role in all of this, we'll try again to work things out."

We returned to his place, unloaded my boxes from his car, and put them back into his garage, which is where they stayed until the end.

3. The Attempt at Counseling

This was huge. He acknowledged his role in the disaster, grudgingly, but he did admit it nonetheless. Based on my modest but renewed hopes of reconciliation, I set up counseling for us with a Christian counseling team to first meet with each of us separately, and then we would all meet together to try to get to the bottom of this. The process would take a total of six hours and cost more than $600, which we split, of course.

Will I be able to put this mess behind me and begin again without the baggage from the past?

What does John need to do to regain my trust? *Will I be able to put this mess behind me and begin again without the baggage from the past? Can we go on with such a shaky foundation?* I had my doubts, but I was certainly willing to try.

I truly loved this man. I remembered all of John's good qualities and all of the good times. Was it possible that after all had transpired to ever get that back again? I was encouraged by the fact that he did acknowledge his role in this fiasco and that he was willing to go to counseling; these were indeed positive signs. He had a very low opinion of counseling and said that we'd spend the entire time talking about traumas from our childhoods. But at least now both of us were working on the relationship, not just me. I took it as a good sign even though he grumbled about going.

I spoke with a female counselor for about an hour and John spoke with a male counselor. Then the four of us got together to wrap up and come to terms with the situation. I explained the entire story to my counselor, and she was dismayed. She asked what I wanted to get out of the session, and I said that I wanted to set up a framework for our relationship going forward based on truth, respect, and open communication. I understand that his chat went along similar lines.

When he got the hint that he would be expected to acknowledge his role in front of three people and propose a way to proceed forward based on the consequences of his actions (intentional or not), he bristled. It was one thing to admit it to me privately in the car on the brink of a breakup, but to admit it to me and two counselors—no way was that happening.

When the four of us convened after our individual sessions, he admitted nothing. Actually, he lied and also got in a few jabs while we were at it.

JOHN: "You should have known what the taxes were before you bought the house."

DONNA MARIE: "Yes, that's true. But the house appreciated substantially so the taxes went up. And I also had no idea about all of the other expenses for bugs, landscaping, and chemicals. When I got the full picture I was ready to sell it—but you interfered."

JOHN:　"Well, you should have known."

DONNA MARIE:　"You interfered in the sale of my house."

JOHN:　"Me? Well, I guess I might have said something…"

Well, I guess I might have said something…

After bullying, badgering, ridiculing, and threatening me to not sell my house for fifteen months, this is what he came up with. He *might* have said "something."

"Reckless words pierce like a sword."
– Proverbs 12;18

So it seemed that all of the soul searching was for naught. We returned to square one. He lied to the counselors about his role. They concluded that, given his obvious lack of cooperation, I would have been better off forcibly evicting him at the beginning. It looked like there was no chance that this relationship could be saved. It seemed that he was much happier pretending that none of this happened; he tried to save face, not the relationship. Looking back, I can only remember how distraught I was over my mother's health. But I placed a very high value on my relationship with him. Who knew that the real estate market in Florida would drop fifty percent and so fast at that? Anyway, all my cash was under the bridge at this point. John was not going to budge. There was no give and take and no respect in this relationship. Yes, he was kind to everyone else, and yes, he used to be kind to me, but now he acted like a true bully.

He sat back and watched smugly while his seeds of destruction took root and sabotaged my retirement.

After the counseling, we had arrived right back where we started. No wait, it was much worse! We exhausted yet another avenue. He had just made a mockery out of our reconciliation, again, with more lies—always more lies. He lied to the counselors. Flip. Flop. Flip. Flop.

He adamantly refused to accept responsibility for his actions right after he acknowledged them. He sat back and watched smugly while his seeds of destruction took root and sabotaged my retirement.

He wanted to simply put it all behind us and start over like nothing had happened. Sure, nothing had happened to him! I guess he wanted another chance to control me and my money and to plan another act of economic exploitation. But I could no longer be fooled; he had lost his power over me. Once again, I could no longer believe a word he uttered.

It is said that man starting lying about one hour after he started talking. In this case especially, it was true. This was not a man that I could even consider marrying. We agreed to break up. *Good, it is finally over. Let's live our lives separately from here on out.* Maybe he can easily find another woman who will buy him a free house, but it won't be me. He should ask her first, not just take it for granted or things might end badly again.

4. No, Wait

Then the e-mails started. Why was I so upset? He wanted to know. After all, he had offered to take care of me. That offer was still on the table. He would make it all up to me. Remember the spreadsheet? *Oh no, not the spreadsheet again!*

He offered again to take care of me, but this time I was beyond skeptical. I would not give up my job and put my financial survival under his control when he already reneged on the same offer once before. I asked for cash up front. But he refused; I guess it was not enough power for Mr. Control.

I said that going forward we could only be buddies, but he didn't listen. He countered that we were not buddies; we were going to be married. Yeah, right! With too many lies, too many dirty tricks, and too little care, there was only half of a couple here; only one of us was trying. I kept giving and he kept taking. I was done giving at this point, but he still wanted to take.

We drifted on a little while longer. We had so many things tied up together: college basketball season tickets, a pre-paid investment seminar, and pre-paid vacations to South Carolina and St. Maarten. After all of this time—twenty-one years now, our lives were very much intertwined.

I had very little anticipation that he would acknowledge, in writing, what he had done or that he would ever rectify what he had done. Short of that, we were over. There was indeed no hope.

Time passed. For the first time in twenty-one years, he forgot my birthday. Was that simply an oversight or was that a message consistent with a pattern of emotional abuse? He no longer lived in my rental house. So I guess there was no reason to even pretend to be nice to me anymore.

5. The Fifth Threat

Time just drifted by. I busily rebuilt my life. I created new connections where I once had none. I forged new friendships with individuals who did not know John.

I busily rebuilt my life. I created new connections where I once had none.

I worked on my professional coaching certification. I was healing. Time passed, and I grew stronger.

By March 2009, the college basketball season ended. We both enjoyed going to the games very much; it was exciting mid-week entertainment. My trips to Florida had become few and far between because of the basketball tickets and a serious lack of interest on my part.

In late March 2009, we attended an investment seminar in West Central Florida that we had pre-paid for the year before. We decided to commute instead of staying in the conference hotel. The sessions were great, but it was a very tiring four days—driving back and forth and spending all day in meetings. We even skipped out on the last day due to overload. I had taken a vacation from work, but I spent the entire time in meetings. I only had one day to relax and enjoy the Florida sunshine because I was due to head north to go back to work, but the weather did not cooperate, so I decided to take a nap.

After I lay down, my fiancé came in to the bedroom, kissed me on the forehead, and said that was my final warning. He did not want to go on like this anymore. *Thanks a lot, Judas, for ruining my nap!*

I got up and packed all of my clothes. That day it was much too late to go to the storage facility; in fact, it was almost time for me to go to the airport. On top of the folded clothes and toiletries, I placed the list of storage places with phone numbers for easy access when it was time. This was ridiculous. He kept threatening me, but he refused to acknowledge his role in the whole fiasco. I gave up; I did not have any feelings of love for him anymore, and it looked like it was truly hopeless. He was not going to make it right after all; he would not try. It was over.

6. It Was Indeed Over

Finally, in May 2009, we had the talk. He said that he waited six months to bring up the subject and that he was not happy with the way we were interacting—so cool and distant. He said that six months before the talk he knew it was over. At Thanksgiving 2008, he asked me to unpack my mother's serving platter, but I offered to buy him a new one instead. Knowing that I was frugal to a fault, he assumed at that moment that things had ended between us.

Knowing that I was frugal to a fault, he assumed at that moment that things had ended between us.

At Christmas, I requested that we not give each other cards or gifts. The thought of buying an "I love you sweetheart" card was more than I could bear. He agreed but then bought me a card anyway. It was awkward. The same thing happened on Valentine's Day. But now, it was time for the talk. All our joint plans and commitments were behind us. I had not planned any new activities with him. He began the conversation.

JOHN: "You are not very affectionate toward me anymore. Something is wrong."

DONNA MARIE: "Well, you sabotaged my retirement. I do not owe you a free house."

JOHN: "I see."

DONNA MARIE: "After you interfered with the initial sale of the house, you also refused to buy half—or we might have made it. But you adamantly refused to buy half, even when given the chance to stay in the house that you loved. And when you had the chance to buy the house all for yourself, you refused to make an offer until I had another offer. Were you trying to make sure that I lost the most money possible?"

JOHN: "No."

He held back on making an offer for the house that he loved more than air. Did he really think that I would cheat the two realtors of their commissions just to give him the house when he wouldn't even make an offer when I desperately needed one?

I reinforced that I no longer loved him. He said that he did not want to be buddies. So what exactly were we still doing together? From then on, we decided we would drift no more.

He blamed me for letting the relationship drag on, even though he said he knew it was over six months before. I was just digging out of the financial hole that he had put me in. Month after month, I saved my money and planned to retire some day, again. I was very busy working full time and training in the evenings as a professional coach. And I was completely numb. He was the one who kept threatening me—why didn't he just go already? He could no longer hurt me emotionally or financially, so not much mattered to me at that point.

He could no longer hurt me emotionally or financially...

In a gallant gesture reminiscent of the good old days of our relationship, he loaded up my boxes in his car, drove them up from Florida, and moved his stuff out of my apartment. He also decided that I could keep the engagement ring and the timeshare; this made up for one-fifteenth of my loss. It was better than nothing; I came very close to ending up with nothing—except my principles and my values.

The devastating betrayal by the person closest to me, at the most vulnerable time of my life, cut a hole in me the size of the Grand Canyon. I felt like I had crawled a mile over broken glass.

The devastating betrayal by the person closest to me, at the most vulnerable time of my life, cut a hole in me the size of the Grand Canyon. I felt like I had crawled a mile over broken glass. Although it was an excruciatingly painful time in my life, I somehow knew that I would survive; this would not be the end of me.

Looking back, there were amazing parallels between the course of my mother's condition and the tortured course of my broken relationship. The two major players in my life at the time were my mother and my man. Is it an odd coincidence that their courses were similar? My mother's condition involved a whole series of wild ups and downs. She went from death's door to being discharged to return home. She went from being fine to terminally ill and back again several times. It was an amazing roller coaster ride for us both.

My relationship took a similarly wild path. We were fine, we got engaged, he sabotaged my retirement, we drifted, we made up, we split, and we reconciled—over and over. While I helped my mother, John hurt me. I don't know whether it is a common occurrence to have these amazing parallels in life. But discovering that my two key relationships took a similar path at approximately the same time was quite remarkable to me—and quite devastating.

7. Possible Rationale for His Actions

"Tough times expose shared values."
– John Haas

Everyone I talk to seems to have a different theory as to how something as bizarre as this could have happened. We were widely viewed as "the perfect couple." Both tall, we danced great together. People would even buy us drinks to keep up the show. We mutually enjoyed an amazing array of activities. I always thought that we were soul mates. To the very end, he went on and on about "loving me so much" and "loving me with all of his heart." Yeah, sure.

Did I ever think that my alleged soul mate would sabotage my retirement, threaten me repeatedly, and destroy our relationship over a building? Not in a million years! Our relationship can be divided into two distinct phases: before the house and after the house. Before the house, things were great. But after he moved into my house, something snapped. An imposter had taken up residence in my fiancé's body! So I guess that he did not love me after all; he only loved his idea of me, the Donna Marie that did what he wanted and that he controlled completely.

We almost saved our relationship several times. But it was not to be. Yes, I did lose a fortune, and my retirement plans went up in smoke. I lost my mother, my man, my money, and my health all at the same time.

How exactly he benefited from all of this is a mystery to me.

But looking at his side, he lost the house, access to my money, and the woman that he so wanted to marry up until the very end. Unless he got a major buzz out of punishing me, the only rationale for his actions appears to be control. How exactly he benefited from all of this is a mystery to me. Where was the payoff for him? I didn't see it then, and I guess I never will. I have no idea what happened, and more importantly, no idea why it happened. Many have offered their thoughts. I have been told that maybe he:

- was merely exhibiting courtship behavior in the good times;
- was acting like a gentleman only to set the trap;
- thought that being engaged meant that he already owned me;
- has a latent or split personality disorder;
- has a defective character lacking integrity;
- is a total control freak;
- is a classic narcissist;
- has early dementia; or
- is simply a jerk.

Some of the misguided amateur psychologist types told me that I actually asked for what happened. Thank you very much, but that was quite unhelpful. (See twenty-one stupid things to say to people at the back of the book.)

But in reality, there was something seriously wrong. He only felt compelled to tell the truth when we were on the brink of disaster. How can a person live like that? That kind of behavior was not real, sustainable, or trustworthy.

Really, it does not matter anymore. It happened; it's over. I have moved on. I have undergone extensive training as an energy leadership and empowerment coach. I do understand that I played a role by having him in my life. Sure, I should have never let him rent my house in the first place. Sure, I should have forcibly evicted him when it was time to retire. As they say, 20/20 hindsight makes for very clear vision. Thank goodness I moved very far from where I was emotionally and spiritually. I now have filled my life so that any future man would be an addition to my life, but he won't *be* my life.

But I also know that through it all, I lived my values. I was true to my character. I treated John like a loving fiancée, even when he treated me like dirt. I can look back and assure myself that I did

...through it all, I lived my values.

what I thought was best for my mother and what I thought was best for our relationship at the time. I thought we could work things out like reasonable adults, just as we had so many times in the past, but I was wrong. Several times we came very close to working it out. It is only in hindsight that everything looks so obviously hopeless.

I tried to hold my conduct to high standards and to treat others as I would like to be treated. I tried to act with integrity and courtesy. I am not a saint, and I am sure that I did plenty of things wrong, but I tried to adhere to the core values that I ascribe to:

- honesty,
- fairness,
- consideration,

- compromise, and

- reconciliation.

He chose not to, but that was his prerogative. But now I realize that my perceptions of his values were clearly in error. What he did is absolutely unfathomable to me; it was downright despicable.

If the roles were reversed, there is no way that this would have happened in the first place. I would never have made demands regarding the disposition of a property that I did not own. And even if somehow it would have happened, I would have seized one of the dozen or so chances to make it right. I can only guess that he adhered to the values that he ascribes to, which are clearly in conflict with mine.

So after he seized the opportunity for economic exploitation, we were not soul mates as I once believed. And we could never have really been a true couple given this huge divergence in our values. What he considered acceptable treatment of me included threats and ridicule, and I considered it intolerable. He killed the golden goose—together no more.

All of this happened while we were only engaged. If he believed that he had the license to verbally and emotionally abuse and control me as his fiancée, I shudder to think what he planned to do to me if we had ever wed. My theory is that he was only good to his ex-wife because he wanted to retain the respect of his children; however, I had no such safety valve to protect me.

I shudder to think what he planned to do to me if we had ever wed.

Every time I think of what happened, I thank God that I did not marry him. If we would have reconciled anywhere along the way, I certainly would have married him. Perhaps the universe protected me from an even worse fate or else perhaps there is something else that I am destined to do. We will see.

I thank God that I did not marry him.

I now try to live a Christian life; I am by no means perfect, but I am making progress. I know that I attempted to do the right thing. Looking back, I know that some will think that I was a fool. But in my mind, I acted like a loving fiancée would. I tried to act like a Christian.

Going head to head, I would never have been able to match his level of lies, deception, and deceit. I was clearly out of my league interacting with him. I am glad for that, and the next man in my life will be glad for that too.

Things are looking up for me already. I am very optimistic. I still have my job and have kicked off a new business. My health has been restored. I have new friends who never knew him. I have connected with long-lost family. My life is back on track. In fact, I am doing very well. I have new opportunities, a new vision, and new plans for my future.

CHAPTER 11

My Recovery Process

*"What if the universe is not conspiring against me? What if it
is actually supporting me—teaching me, leading me?"*
– Aurora Winter

1. My Physical Recovery

*"Success requires persistence, the ability
not to give up in the face of failure…"*
– Martin Seligman

Between the time that I wanted to sell my house in September 2005 and the time I actually sold my house in May 2008, my weight ballooned up another twenty pounds. I am five feet eight inches tall, medium build, and can carry a little weight, but not this much. Given that I was already somewhat dissatisfied with my weight, which was already almost twenty pounds above my ultra-trim weight before all of this started, I was truly distraught. At that point, nearly forty pounds heavier than I would've liked, I found I could only squeeze into two of my business suits. A classic emotional eater, I felt threatened so I ate; I guess it helped me to feel more secure.

I barely noticed while all of this happened, and the pounds packed on. I was not very "aware"; I was not living in the present. I was under extreme stress from multiple sources. So I ate for comfort, and I ate to escape. I realized that I was conducting a relationship with food. How sad was that? When the world closed in on me, food had become my closest companion. It was pathetic.

I ate for comfort, and I ate to escape.

- I felt trapped, so I ate.

- I felt betrayed, so I ate.

- I felt alone, so I ate.

- I felt unloved, so I ate.

- I felt sad, so I ate.

- I felt bad, so I ate.

- I wanted to avoid my pain, so I ate.

- I desperately wanted my needs to be met, so I ate.

- I couldn't face my loss, so I ate.

- I was unable to cope, so I ate.

I had so many triggers. According to Dr. Robert Anthony's research, food had become my support system, my crutch. Fear made me fat. I substituted food for friendship and love. Food answered the distress I felt for my pain, stress, loss, and worry. I self-medicated with food; I formed my deepest connection with food. Food seemed so harmless and necessary. How had this gotten so far out of control without me noticing it when it was happening?

Now all of a sudden, I was up forty pounds from my ideal ultra-trim weight. But all of this excess food somehow did little to meet my emotional needs after all. Worse than that, my excess weight sapped my confidence even more. My appearance became an outward sign that I was indeed in trouble. I tried to hide all of my troubles from everyone, but my weight was right there in 3-D for all the world to see.

...my weight was right there in 3-D for all the world to see.

I used food as a substitute for the relationship that I lost. I lounged around in sweat pants. Ah yes, the elastic waistband was indeed an enabler; it kept expanding with me just like a true friend.

I was oblivious until my weight slapped me in the face one day when I had to get a new picture ID for work; the previous ID was five years old. The new picture showed a very chubby-cheeked Donna Marie that I did not wish to accept. *Oh no! What happened to me?*

I truly gained a lot of weight during my trials and tribulations; my face looked like a balloon. I guess I gained the weight very fast. But this was not acceptable. My waistline had completely vanished; put out an APB—I have got to find it again.

> *My waistline had completely vanished; put out an APB…*

The sale of the house, even though it had catastrophic consequences for my finances, truly helped my emotional and physical wellbeing. It was over and time to move forward. I had reached bottom, but at least I had no more doubts. With hard work, I would dig out of this. I achieved financial independence once; I could do it again. I could no longer vacillate back and forth and round and round. My money was gone. There was no bailout in the works for me. I was not too big to fail—financially anyway; I was too insignificant to be noticed. It was over. It was finished. I was on my own. I had to recognize this and move forward. I would no longer experience panic attacks or debilitating stress. My body was ready to heal.

> *I was not too big to fail…*

From the depths of despair where I suffered a pinched nerve in my neck and a right hand that I could not use, I am pleased to report that I've now reached 99 percent physical recovery. Today I have lost more than thirty pounds; more is on the way. I play tennis—no better or worse than I did before. I ramped up my endurance to in-line skate nine miles in Miami Beach and to skate a half-marathon in Chicago. The skating has even helped my endurance for tennis, and it is reshaping my body in a good way.

I bike on trails and kayak on local rivers. I line dance and ballroom dance; my Viennese waltz is much improved. I play golf; well, I should really say that I swing the clubs. But what a difference! I have my life back. I have always been very athletic, but this ordeal really set me back.

People ask me how I went from almost being immobilized with a serious neck injury to stronger, thinner, and more fit than I was before, even as my age is advancing. I can only relay what worked for me. You might need to adapt it to work for you.

Key Steps in My Physical Recovery

The key steps in my recovery were to:

1. Tame the pain: At the time of my acute injury, taming the pain was the first key step. When you hurt every minute of the day, it is difficult to make progress on any other dimension of recovery. I took as many pain pills as I needed but not one more. And I cut back on them as soon as I was able.

2. Assemble the right team: I searched for doctors and other health care providers who understood both my injury and my state of mind. Only those providers truly helped me. It was important to work as a team in my recovery. My pain doctor and my physical therapist were truly amazing cheerleaders for me. I'm grateful to them.

3. Get enough sleep: I was in major pain with pins and needles running down my right arm and hand 24/7. It was difficult to get to sleep and to stay asleep. Your body does much of its healing when you sleep. And when you sleep, you do not think about your pain or your limitations. Sleep is truly a precious gift.

4. Calm my thoughts: After the medical dream team was in place and I did not have to fight the system to take sick leave, obtain pain pills, or have essential physical therapy sessions, I was then able to get my mental house in order to calm my thoughts and set the tone for my recovery.

5. Adopt a recovery attitude: After the acute crisis subsided somewhat and I was in a proper course of treatment, I changed my mind set. I was indeed going to recover, no question about it. That realization changed everything for me. Let's be clear here. I am not Christopher Reeve or Bruce Schneider who probably adopted this as Step 1. I am just an average person who faced multiple major crises in my life at the same time. Changing my attitude at this stage changed my life and set the course for my physical recovery. Better late than never, right?

   I was indeed going to recover, no question about it...

6. Commit one hundred percent: I totally committed to my recovery. Nothing would stand in my way—not traction, painful exercises, relapses, pain, more pins and needles, or a troublesome second spinal injection. Nothing was going to keep me down. I was one hundred percent committed to my recovery, no matter what.

7. Do isometrics: In any exercise plan, there are so-called good exercises (the ones you don't mind doing), and there are the so-called bad exercises (the ones you hate doing). The isometrics that I hated gave me the best results, so I did more than my share of them to accelerate and intensify my recovery.

8. Seek comfort: I sought comfort in my precious late cat, Katie. She truly was a wonderful friend to me.

9. Be persistent: As I improved, I gradually increased my work hours from half days to full days. All the while, the sick leave monitors for my employer and the medical insurance provider grew antsy. They wanted me back to work full time with no more PT. Well, I was barely functional. I worked a full day and went straight home to bed to get ready to do it again. Was this living? According to the monitor and the insurance provider, yes, it was. I repeatedly petitioned for additional time, took some abuse, and finally arranged for more therapy as well as special sessions for my right hand. And that my friends, as they say, made all of the difference.

10. Build upon the gains: After I was finally functional, I decided that I wanted to be optimal. I worked and I trained and I worked some more. Skating thirteen miles was a major achievement, and now my sights are on even higher goals.

11. Reach for the dream goal: After I shed the first twenty pounds of excess weight, which was truly remarkable for me, I did not stop there. My weight had plateaued. I've heard that women in their fifties CANNOT lose weight no matter how little they eat. But I was going to be the exception; I skated 66 miles over six days and ate like a rabbit. The result—I lost two itty, bitty pounds, yes only two measly pounds! So, undaunted, I went on Nutrisystem for the final twenty and the results were nothing short of amazing, you'll see.

And here I am today; I am active, and I am fit. I lost a bunch of weight. I can run up five flights of stairs in heels. From the depths of despair and ten months of treatment, I returned triumphant. Is that cool or what?

From the depths of despair and ten months of treatment, I returned triumphant.

When I can, I skate nine miles a day after work. To extend my season, my temperature limit for outdoor skating is an aggressive 40 degrees with wind chill; below that it is just plain too painful. I learned that the hard way when I trained for a street skate in Miami in February 2009. It sounded like a good idea. Skating in Miami Beach in February? Sure. But I did not factor in that I would need to train in the north in December and January—brr!

How did I manage the training under less than ideal conditions? I did it with focus, persistence, determination, and flannel. My goal was to skate six miles in Miami Beach; I had never skated that far before. Actually I had no idea how far I could skate because I never measured it; up to that point, I just skated for fun. To train, I went to a local high school track and went round and round and round, eventually working up to twenty-four laps or six miles. How absolutely boring—going around a quarter-mile track is way beyond mind-numbing!

But even more importantly, it was a new rubberized track with almost no roll at all. Each time I took a stride, I went about three feet and then had to take another stride. Unbeknownst to me, I was over-training. Who knew? So when I got to the Miami Beach street skate and they mixed up the short skate details, the six-mile skate turned into a nine-mile skate, and I did it without a hitch. I was so proud of that accomplishment. It was my first organized street skate, and I did it.

2. My Financial Recovery

"Life is short and so is money."
– Bertolt Brecht

Between the time that I wanted to sell my house to net $650,000 and when I actually sold my house to net $340,000, my monthly net worth statement was in a free fall. For more than two years before my early retirement date, I prepared a detailed net worth statement each month to track my progress until the big day in November 2005. I added up all of my investments, cash, IRAs, rollovers, pension, real estate, and other assets to assess my financial readiness. I had no debt. Things looked good. *Look out, tennis courts; here I come!* I thought.

But it was not to be. So how did I dig myself out of this mess? The most important aspect of my financial recovery was my job. I thank God every day that I did not give up my job. I came very close to quitting when the fairness spreadsheet was put into play, but it never got that far. Perhaps someone was watching over me after all.

The basic tenets of accumulating wealth applied to my case as in every other: earn more, spend less, or do both. The two key features of my financial recovery plan were to work and save. Work and save. Work and save.

> *...earn more, spend less, or do both.*

Key Steps in My Financial Recovery

The key steps in my financial recovery were to:

1. Work longer: I have postponed my retirement approximately five years. Yes, it is a bummer. John was certainly not worth it. But working longer has taken away my fears of financial insecurity. I did not want to spend the rest of my life thinking, *I could have had that, if only he hadn't highjacked my house...* No way am I going to live like that. I will be whole when I retire one way or another.

2. Start a business: I kicked off a business to generate income in my retirement years. I calculated that $10,000 in annual net income from my business equates to $200,000 in capital at 5 percent interest. So with extra income from my business, I don't need to save the entire $370,000 that I lost. And I paid the start-up costs of the new business from my full-time job, thus smoothing over the lean early days of a new business venture.

3. Live economically: I now live in a small apartment close to work. All utilities and repairs are included, so there are no additional costs, ever. They even replace the light bulbs, no kidding. I paid a pet deposit for my cat, but I do not pay the dreaded pet rent. My commute is short. Living close to work saves on gas and subway fares. My apartment is a much smaller living space than I am used to, but I am single-mindedly saving for my retirement again.

4. Spend less on entertainment: Because John and I went out all the time to dinner, the movies, the theater, dancing, college basketball games, and pro baseball games, I saved a lot of money when that stopped. I spend about $5,000 less a year on entertainment now. I have a DVR that provides much entertainment flexibility with friends.

5. Spend less on travel: By not traveling back and forth to Florida every other weekend, I save about $6,000 a year.

6. Spend less on clothes: I am in pure retirement saving mode. If I don't need it, and I mean *need* it, then I don't buy it. I did buy some clothes to launch my first book in 2010, but I consider that advancing my business.

7. Eat lunch in: I was doing this before to some degree, but now it is a serious commitment. I eat soup in for about $2 a day vs. $10 a day to eat in the cafeteria. This adds up to a total savings of more than $1,500 per year, depending upon the number of days I am in the office.

8. Pay off credit cards: Interest charges and fees do not get me closer to retirement, so they are not part of my plan. I pay my balances in full, every time, every month.

9. Cut variable costs everywhere else: I clip coupons, shop for sales, and don't buy what I don't need. My long-term goals are much more important than any short-term splurges. My goal is to get my net worth and projected income back to where it was in 2005, this time counting on the ongoing income from my business.

My long-term goals are much more important than any short-term splurges.

10. Keep the end game in sight: This can be summed up very simply: When in doubt, don't.

Keep the end game in sight…

Between working longer and spending less, I am well on my way. My revised retirement goal is in sight. I will be just fine. I am making lemonade out of lemons. After all, what was the alternative? I refuse to wallow in self-pity. I am once again beginning to plan my retirement date, and I have started to run my monthly net worth statement again. Before it was simply too depressing. But now it is exciting once again as I rebuild my retirement capital and get closer and closer to the end date again.

How did I manage that? I did it with focus, persistence, and determination. My goal is to retire with approximately the same amount of money that I had in 2005. Here are some of the steps that I took:

- I found out how much capital I needed—the gap.

- I calculated my earnings each month, net of taxes, health insurance, pension, and other required deductions.

- I estimated how much of the net income went toward fixed costs such as rent, cable, car expenses, food, health and beauty, long-term care insurance, church, charity, contingencies, and other semi-fixed costs.

- I estimated how much of the net could be applied for variable expenses. Even though I am saving for retirement, I still need to relax, take a break, and indulge here and there.

- I estimated how much of the net could go toward savings.

- I tried to be as realistic as possible so my checkbook and credit card statements helped identify spending patterns and unforeseen items that crop up.

- I calculated how many months it would take based on my new net savings. I factored in limited returns on my existing investments, which are held conservatively. I have lost so much money that I have run for cover; I will work on that issue later in the case of the dreaded double dip recession.

- I calculated the annual income that I will need to earn in retirement to meet my passive and active income goals for the next thirty years.

Once again, my retirement date is in sight. See that, I can't be held down! This mix of strategies and concrete action steps has brought me back into the retirement game. Yes, it is not the same as my original retirement plan. But realism and flexibility are hallmarks of successful retirees going forward—and better late than never.

This mix of strategies and concrete action steps has brought me back into the retirement game.

Even with everything that has happened to me, I consider myself very fortunate. My losses began a long time ago, as Florida led the real estate crash. Since then, the losses around the country have become much more widespread. Many couples have simply weathered the storm by staying in their homes, underwater, and maintaining their loving relationships. But others have lost their jobs and their homes and have been devastated. Many others experienced much larger losses than I have, some even catastrophic.

I express deep gratitude for my financial recovery and the blessings and opportunities in my life.

So yes, I am indeed one of the lucky ones who still have a stable job that has helped me dig out of the mess that I was in. And I also had and took the opportunity to kick off a new business to help keep my cash flow positive into my early retirement years and maybe for many years to come. I express deep gratitude for my financial recovery and the blessings and opportunities in my life.

3. My Emotional Recovery

"Doing your best at this moment puts you in the best place for the next moment."
– Oprah Winfrey

My emotional recovery was a tortuous and non-linear process. I discovered early on in my journey that I was not a very "aware" person. Who knew? Just how does an unaware person realize that they are unaware?

Just how does an unaware person realize that they are unaware?

So busy working and advancing my career, I did not take the time to become aware of the present. I also lived for the future. I put my life on hold so that I could work hard, so that I could retire early. I lost thirty-eight years in between.

First, never in a million years did I think that I would be in an abusive and controlling relationship. I was normally smart and independent—except when my mother was in her final days. They say that you end up with a man like your father, but John was not like that for the first sixteen years. The contrast could not have been greater. John absolutely worshipped his daughter, and he gave her a four-year free ride through college. My father thought that

...never in a million years did I think that I would be in an abusive and controlling relationship.

girls were a complete waste of time, and not only did he not pay for one dime of my college expenses, but he also tried to block me from going at all.

No, for the first sixteen years, John was nothing like my father; after we got engaged, it was a different story altogether. He sure fooled me and everyone else—before something snapped, before he became a completely different person brazenly pretending that he owned my house.

The loss of my mother, my man, and my money all at the same time was catastrophic for me. The cuts were very deep. As I have been told, I was ill-equipped from childhood to place a high value on myself. After all, my father thought girls were useless. He never let an opportunity pass where he did not remind me of that fact. So I worked very hard at my career to somehow increase my own perception of my value—at least monetarily.

I saw my value only in doing but not my value in being. I looked outside of myself to be valued. And I found John, the man who became my fiancé after sixteen years as my companion. He said that he loved me and stuck by me through the many tough times before that fateful house. Our relationship wasn't always perfect. Nine years in, we broke up for six months. But we worked things out satisfactorily.

From then on for some reason, I was completely convinced that he was to be the man in my life forever. At the time, I thought the messages were divinely inspired. Now I guess I didn't know the difference among the many random thoughts swirling around in my head.

This ordeal truly shook me to my very core. My fiancé was the center of my life before things headed south, my best friend, and my soul mate. I loved him more than I could ever express. I so wanted to share the rest of my life with him. Emotionally committed to the relationship, I did not consider for a moment that things would not work out between us. In my mind, there was mutual respect, but now that looks like an illusion. I stood ready to do what it took to make things work. I was in way too deep and had subordinated too many of my needs and too much of my identity for there to be an "us."

But what did I miss? What subtle cues did I not detect? Was I so busy assuming that things would work out that I missed the signs? People tell me there had to be signs. What patterns fell into place unbeknownst to me because I had a low level of "awareness"? What did I miss because I wanted everything to work out? Only after we were engaged did his true self emerge. He thought that the deal had been sealed, that he was home free (pun intended).

Throughout the good years, John validated me both as a person and as a woman. I relied on him to meet many of my emotional and relational needs. That mistake cost me dearly, if only I had loved myself more. My crash was far worse than it should have been because I was so *...if only I had loved myself more.* dependent upon him for my validation. I needed to find other ways to meet my emotional needs than with busyness, food, and John. Ironically, I had planned to greatly broaden my circle of friends after I retired and had a lot more free time, but alas, I never got the chance.

In so deep, I started to physically shake at the thought of living without him. I was emotionally dependent upon him to the point of having physical withdrawal symptoms at the mere thought of a split. The utter emptiness that I would feel without him was unfathomable and had to be avoided at all costs. But alas, although I was in one hundred percent, I discovered that he was in ten percent—both emotionally and financially. Oh sure, he still "loved" me. But his brand of controlling "love" was clearly unacceptable. Oh! How I wish he would have run off with a sassy Argentine instead of plundering my retirement savings.

Controlling men go through the motions of love, but they primarily focus on themselves. This became painfully obvious when the dialogues about the house took place. I only wish I knew what I was dealing with at the time; things might have worked out very differently. I did do the right thing in eventually putting my house on the market, but I was so overwhelmed by my mother's illness that I was not able to process two major life-altering situations simultaneously.

Was he really just waiting all of those years to grab my money? Is that possible or even plausible? Was he really just waiting for his chance to control me and my money after he set the trap? Or was it simply a case of opportunism when he moved into my house, took control, and did not know how to reverse course and save face? Could it be a mix? Did he truly move to Florida to sell his business? Or did he really move there just to play golf year round and slyly

The good news is that he sprung the trap before I was caught in it.

use the sale of his business as a cover story so that I would agree? I will never know. The good news is that he sprung the trap before I was caught in it.

As I said, I was out of my league with all of the lies, dirty tricks, and dirty deeds. Silly me, I took everything at face value. I must have looked like a lamb going to the slaughter—easy pickings indeed.

My mother's repeated crises and long-term decline set the perfect stage for him to make his move on my money and play his game of economic exploitation. I was so consumed by my mother's care, I guess I did not pay close enough attention to him and his actions. In his defense, he helped me a great deal with my mother's arrangements and all of the moving in and out of the hospital. So I was completely blindsided by his deception.

He took full advantage of the worst crisis of my life to make his move. Who cares if my mother's health was dramatically declining? Who cares if I stood by him and supported him when both of his parents were dying? I can only imagine how disappointed his parents would be at John's selfish, deceitful stunt against a woman, his fiancée no less. I am not a psychologist. I do not know the answers. I look back and wonder how he could possibly have done this to me at the worst time of my life. But it was the perfect time for him to make his move. I guess that he was assured that I could not possibly lose both my mother and lose him at the same time so he grew more aggressive, which is when the threats began.

Only the first threat worked though. The subsequent threats merely drove a deeper and deeper wedge between us.

Only the first threat worked though. The subsequent threats merely drove a deeper and deeper wedge between us.

Sadly, he only needed the first threat to work in order to successfully sabotage my retirement plans.

When I finally put the house on the market, he could no longer control me. I knew that I had done everything I could. By then, I was in action mode; I was looking out for myself. That gave me some strength and momentum to keep going.

I guess that, according to his line of thinking, if he could not control me and my money, then he needed to punish me. He actually lost the house that he wanted just so that he could hurt me more. I am not a psychologist, but that truly sounds sick. He would never let go under any circumstances. The tenacious pit bull had been unleashed and would never let go. Was the engagement the trigger where he finally felt free to be himself after all the years of suppression? I will never know.

You may find the following steps that I took helpful as well:

1. Accept the situation: No sense in denying it, my fiancé highjacked my house. It happened. I accept that. I wish that it weren't true, but it is.

2. Stop the damage: As soon as I realized that he was completely intransigent, I put my house on the market. He could no longer control me, and with that action, I had done all that I could do to start protecting myself and my assets.

3. Make reasonable offers: When he was livid that I was giving the house away at $635,000, I offered to stay if he bought half the house.

4. Consider reasonable offers: When he, for a very brief moment in time, accepted full responsibility for his actions, he offered to take care of me until I was 62. I accepted.

5. Read self-help books and blogs and listen to inspiring CDs and MP3s: I was particularly impressed by positive thinking. This formed the basis of my journey into being aware of a different way of thinking when I needed it most. I accept myself as a precious creature that is loved by God.

6. Make other connections: I found new friends and connected with long-lost family to build a support network for the first time in my life.

7. Train as a professional coach: I was so energized by the inspiring books and CDs that I knew I had to learn more, much more. I became a Certified Professional Coach in Bruce Schneider's IPEC program, which offered amazing insights into the power of emotions, levels of energy, limiting beliefs, the nature of thoughts and feelings, and the need for purposeful action. I never considered simply "being"; I was always busy "doing." The IPEC program changed my life and also brought me in contact with many fascinating people.

8. Seek comfort: I found solace in my late cat, Katie—what a wonderful friend. According to Albert Schweitzer: *"There are two means of refuge from the miseries of life: music and cats."* I agree.

9. Lose the shame: I forgave myself and talked about my loss to everyone that I could. Aurora Winter, the Grief Coach, really inspired me. I did not even realize that I was experiencing grief, only loss. I accepted her suggestion in a teleclass to write my story, which helped me enormously; it was included in the best-selling paperback *Bouncing Back: Thriving in Changing Times*. I encourage you to write about your loss too; it really works.

I forgave myself and talked about my loss to everyone that I could.

10. Assemble a support team: I sought out coaches, friends, and others to help and guide me. You know who you can count on.

11. Find as many opportunities to completely relax as you can; complete relaxation clears harmful stress from your body. And laugh as much as you can; laughter is quite a healing tool.

12. Plan a new future: I articulated a new vision for my life, and I envisioned a new dream. I would be okay. And better yet, my plans were no longer limited by his restrictions; I could now live in Santa Barbara if I chose. Are earthquakes better than hurricanes?

13. Forgive and forget: For the first few weeks, the first words out of my mouth when I awoke every morning at 6:00 a.m. to go to work

(long after I should have been retired) were "I hate you!" spoken in a guttural fury right out of the *The Exorcist*. I guess he would be pleased that he left such a lasting legacy. But now it no longer matters; it is all in the past, and I have left the past behind.

14. Take action on passions and make it happen: I started a new business—Goals In Action, LLC—to help others. Starting up and training for my new business was quite demanding and always exciting. It took an enormous amount of time, which helped me to divert my attention from my loss when I needed to.

15. Complete the healing: Move past the situation one hundred percent. I made the decision to let the old feelings go. I had a rule: If it was not helping me in some dimension of my recovery or my new future, then I had to get rid of

> *I made the decision to let the old feelings go.*

it. Even writing this book has helped me to break free of some of the old remaining chains of the past. I hope that the book helps you too.

Now I go out with friends. Obviously it is not the same as having a close romantic relationship; I do miss that part. Someday, I will date again. But because the relationship that I was totally committed to appears to be a complete fraud, I am not sure that my radar is up to speed. I obviously have more work to do on myself. I will take my time.

I believe that my true soul mate will enter my life when I am ready for him. I am changing every day for the better. I believe that there is a man out there who can truly love me, a woman with a bounding joy for life. In the meantime, I am having fun living my new life, sharing my gifts with others, building my business, expressing gratitude for the opportunity, and serving my God.

"I just haven't met you yet."
– Michael Bublé

4. My Spiritual Recovery

"God visits us, but most of the time we are not at home."
– French Proverb

There was a deep void for most of my life. I tried to fill the emptiness with work, a close companion, and emotional eating. I rarely lived in the present. I either worried about the future or fretted about the past. I rarely enjoyed the now. I searched for acceptance and approval from others and many times I received neither. None of these outlets could truly meet my needs. I felt a vast emptiness inside of me. I did not know how the answers that I was looking for would come to me.

When I went off to college, I stopped going to church. Raised in a turbulent household, I did not believe that there was indeed a higher power looking out for me; it seemed implausible. As an adult, I lost my spiritual connection.

I reclaimed that connection when I was visiting my mother in the ICU. That is when I began to reconnect with my faith. I looked for guidance and for more meaning and purpose in my life. Taking care of my mother was the mission that I believe I was called to do. Our roles had clearly reversed.

If you've experienced elder care, you will be familiar with the concept of coming full circle—when you start taking care of the people who took care of you. It is quite unsettling when you first adopt the parental role yourself. After a while, it became clear that being my mother's advocate was my new call to service. I had not fully appreciated just how many times she had been my advocate in the past; thank you, Mom. I wanted to give her the best care that I could because I know that is what she did for me a half a century earlier. When things were completely out of control medically, I sought guidance through my faith.

...being my mother's advocate was my new call to service.

I began to pray and then pray some more. I did not pray for a specific outcome but for strength to see me through the roller coaster of emotions, the conflicting advice, and the uncertain prognoses. I prayed that I could be the best advocate that my mother could have—the way that she was always there for me. Prayer was an essential component in my spiritual recovery.

Prayer was an essential component in my spiritual recovery.

To help build the foundation of my newfound faith, I took Reverend Jenny Cannon's Disciple Bible class where we read the Bible from cover to cover.

Although quite an undertaking, I found it a very powerful exercise, which grounded me in the tenets of the Christian faith straight from the source. The small-group discussions guided by Reverend Jenny made the text come alive. Even though I traveled extensively during this time, I managed to keep up with the readings.

It turns out that my spirit was starving; I had been off track for most of my adult life.

It turns out that my spirit was starving; I had been off track for most of my adult life. The prayers and the Bible study were my first steps to recommit to God in a meaningful way. I believe that I am still in the early days in my spiritual journey, but I know that now I am on the right track in my faith. The spiritual recovery process that I went through helped me to find the strength to go on when four dimensions of my life crashed at the same time.

Key Steps to Spiritual Recovery

The steps I took in my spiritual recovery were to:

1. Reach out in prayer: Prayer helped me to cope during the darkest days, and prayer now helps me to navigate through the uncertainties of life.

2. Surrender to the Lord: I am no longer tied to specific outcomes of my choosing; I no longer think that I am in control.

3. Read the Bible: Reverend Jenny's Disciple class was illuminating and set me on the right path for learning and discovery. I continue to this day.

4. Review other spiritual readings: I subscribe to multiple sources including Moody Bible, Joyce Meyer, and Rick Warren to receive inspirational and faith-based messages that I can apply in my daily life.

5. Seek forgiveness: I asked God to forgive my sins and to guide me in living a more loving, generous, and compassionate Christian life.

6. Express gratitude: I am grateful for my gifts, and I share them freely with others. Having

Having been to some of the poorest countries, I know that we are blessed beyond measure.

been to some of the poorest countries, I know that we are blessed beyond measure.

7. Help others: I offer free coaching for members of my church and offer my services when and where I can.

8. Give to charity: I carefully selected World Vision, Doctors without Borders, Smile Train, and my church to receive the majority of my charitable gifts.

9. Act with compassion: I am shifting from a high-power, type-A professional to a non-judgmental citizen of the world. I appreciate the differences in people and treat them with care. I forgive others.

10. Schedule quiet time: Solitude is a powerful mechanism to connect to divine inspiration. It is not quite meditation. During these sessions, I do not pray, I listen.

When I found God, I discovered the fatherly love that I had not been able to find on earth. I know that my Heavenly Father values and loves me in a way that my earthly father would not and could not. As it turns out, I had to lose everything to discover what truly matters.

5. Entrepreneurship in My Recovery

"Finding your entrepreneurial spirit and making it strong is more important than the idea or business you are developing."
– Robert Kiyosaki

After working for more years in corporate settings than I care to admit, I had the opportunity to start my own business. Just the thought of being an entrepreneur and venturing out on my own was exciting. The sky was the limit. In the back of my mind, I wondered if I could do it—on the inside, I knew that I could. And now I had the chance to make it happen.

The road to this point was long with several twists and turns. A management consultant for more than sixteen years, I paid my dues at PricewaterhouseCoopers and Booz Allen, and I worked in local and regional firms. I built my credentials with an MBA, CPA, and PhD.

Starting a Business: I Can Do This

Starting my own business was exciting. I had been advising many different types of businesses with excellent results for numerous years; now it was my turn to give it a whirl. I prepared to learn how it was done in actual practice. I researched what I needed to learn to get started.

First, I became a Certified Professional Coach both for my personal recovery and to offer helpful services to others. I took a great social media course to learn how to use the Web 2.0 tools to market my business; an information products course to design, package, and market products to enhance my business; a publicity course to tailor my messages; and an excellent show-host training course to kick off my new radio and web TV series. I believed that these are the tools that I needed, in addition to my prior business strategy experience, to kick off a successful new business.

Evolution of the Business Strategy

I crafted a business plan and selected my target markets. I changed the plan three times and decided to self-finance the business using the boot-strap model, that is, using my own money. The plan was to keep working in my full-time job until I could develop multiple sustainable revenue streams. That is what I advised some of my clients to do, so it was a natural choice for me in starting my own business. My recent financial history sealed the deal. I wanted no debt! Because it can take as long as twelve months to generate significant sales and cash flow, the bootstrap model can be a low-stress option for a business startup.

...the bootstrap model can be a low-stress option for a business startup.

This financing model works for some businesses and not for others. There is no one-size-fits-all approach to business startups. The financing scheme for a small business also needs to align with the entrepreneur's risk tolerance. Having just survived enormous financial, emotional, and physical setbacks in my life, I knew the bootstrap model was right for me.

My favorite business area involves working with entrepreneurs to fully monetize their online businesses. I help the clients' website concepts generate more sales and opportunities from their content. Many entrepreneurs have discovered that it is easy to give things away on the web. Somewhere along the line though, entrepreneurs need to start charging a fair price for their products, services, and content in order to have a viable business. I've found many entrepreneurs who are reluctant to charge a fair price for their products, but I help them fix that.

Even though I know that a single-pronged business strategy is the key to launching a successful business, I was called to take a two-pronged approach—at least temporarily. It's funny when you don't take your own advice. But I have a reason. I will execute both business strategies—just sequentially, one before the other. Personal recovery from loss is the first priority; working with entrepreneurs is the second.

Personal recovery from loss is the first priority...

Rationale for the Business

I had not set out to start a business at all. I planned to retire early at 53, marry my long-time companion, and sit back and live the good life. But there was an unforeseen turn in the road for me—brought about indirectly by the real estate crash in Florida. But now I was making the best of the situation. I came out of the steep losses I incurred with a new definition of myself and my retirement. I was alone now. So if I was not going to be skating and playing tennis all day, then what? How could I serve? What was my mission?

I reasoned that many of my financial concerns could be allayed by having income streams in retirement that I could control by doing things that I loved to do—speaking, teaching, coaching, and writing. Isn't that perfect?

Helping Me, Helping Others

But this business has turned out to be far more than a way to fund my new breed of retirement. By motivating me to seek out, learn, and connect with others in varied venues, my business has enabled me to do amazing things. I am helping others and helping myself at the same time. I get to meet incredible people who I would not have met otherwise. Each time I am lifted up and my circle expands. I have met more amazing people in the past year than I have met in my entire life.

I am helping others and helping myself at the same time.

It is heartening to note that my story has impacted others. They feel inspired by my persistence and my determination and that spurs me on. I have bounced back, and I'm helping others to do the same.

Key Steps to Entrepreneurship

The steps I took toward entrepreneurship were to:

1. Set up a company: Goals in Action, LLC became the entity for my business.

2. Train to become a Certified Professional Coach: Although I was a management consultant for most of my career, coaching training provided me with a powerful new set of tools and skills.

3. Learn about social media marketing, information products, media, and publicity: Set up social media accounts on Facebook, Twitter, Linked In, and others.

4. Build a basic website as a major communications vehicle to market my business.

5. Publish a series of mini-blogs in both text and audio podcasts that focus on: Relationships, Happiness & Joy, Hope & Help, Faith & Forgiveness, and Living Your Values. They can be located on the web at http://www.BouncingBackfromLoss.com/blog

6. Reach out to others for joint ventures, connections, and networking opportunities. Partnership dramatically extends my reach.

7. Define a multi-tier product strategy beginning with a free e-book. Develop strategies to maximize and leverage my product line with books, CDs, audios, videos, teleclasses, and coaching programs.

8. Train on audio and video production and show hosting and set up the "Bouncing Back Now" channel on Blog Talk Radio and the "BouncingBackNow" channel on YouTube.

9. Build an interactive "Bouncing Back Community" to share experiences and life lessons with like-minded people.

10. Develop an integrated marketing, communications, and publicity strategy.

11. Trademark my company slogan: Just Say No To The Status Quo™.

12. Execute the business, marketing, and communication strategies and refine as needed.

My business is my passion and is now *elemental* in my recovery.

- If starting a business is not your thing, then I encourage you to seek out your passion so that you can find your joy now.

    ◊ Find an activity that inspires you and that you truly enjoy.

    ◊ Find an area where you are especially skilled.

    ◊ Find an unmet need and go meet it.

- If starting your own business would light your fire, then come on down and get dreaming and planning. If you're not sure what direction to go in, here are a few key questions for you to consider.

Key Questions for a Business Startup

- What is your passion?
- What are your strengths?
- What have people always commended you on?
- What are your interests?
- What do you enjoy doing?
- What gives meaning to your life?
- Do you have role models doing the same thing?
- Do you have a network of resources to tap into?
- What would you be proud to accomplish?
- How much time do you want to put in and for how long?
- What level of risk is acceptable?
- Can you delay gratification to survive the startup phase?
- What business models would you consider?
- Are you seeking consulting contracts?
- Do you want to work independently?

- Five years from now, what would you be doing happily?
- What is your target market?
- Where is there demand?
- What is your unique value proposition?
- What products or services are your target market looking for? How do you know?
- What prices are they willing to pay? How do you know?
- Does the price they are willing to pay enable you to make an acceptable profit margin?
- What products or services would you offer?
- How would you price your products and services?
- What level of competition would you face?
- What is your competitive advantage?
- How can you differentiate to provide excellent customer service?
- How committed are you to paying close attention to details?
- Do you know how to reach a key segment of your market in targeted communications?
- How much capital do you need to run for eighteen months?
- Where will you get the money?
- Have you prepared a detailed business plan?
- How solid are your marketing skills?
- How solid are your technical skills?
- How solid are your management skills?
- How solid are your computer skills?
- How solid are your administration skills?
- What can you do on your own and what can you delegate?
- What is best for you to do and what is best to outsource?

Remember to: Just Say No To The Status Quo™. Apply that principle. Live that principle. Good luck to you if you are starting a business. It is very demanding and time consuming, but exciting nonetheless.

CHAPTER 12

Lessons Learned

*"In order to be happy, we need to both find meaning and pleasure—
to have both a sense of purpose and the experience of emotions."*
– Tal Ben-Shahar

Over the course of my loss and my recovery, I've learned many lessons that I would like to share with you. I can only hope that these might help you to avoid some of the mistakes that I have made.

1. Career and Priority Lessons Learned

"Moderation in all things."
– Andria Terence

I am a woman from a rough-and-tumble, blue-collar background. I had no mentors or role models. Just going to college was huge for me—I was the first in my family—even as the youngest and only girl. I have been chasing success and swimming upstream all of my life.

A workaholic, I tried to find my value by diving headlong into work. I tried to demonstrate to myself that I could be successful in the world; I tried to prove my father wrong. But my addictive personality took hold and never let go. The more I worked, the higher I moved and the more I was expected to work. It was quite a rush to be recognized for my achievements and to reap the financial rewards.

Along the way, many have tried to derail me and to stop me—men and women alike. Many believed that I did not belong in their exclusive club. I swam with the sharks and have the cuts to prove it. Many tried to keep me down and to push me aside—some with grace, some not. Yet, here I am.

For all of the naysayers, there were always those who believed in me, my skills, and my abilities, and who recognized my passion and my contributions. My commitment to clients and my drive for results was always paramount; and it was widely recognized.

My goal entailed starting to live a real life when I reached retirement. It seemed to make sense to me; I was afraid to let up, scared to take my eye off the ball any earlier. If I did not give one hundred percent, I was afraid that I would fail. I don't know why, but I likened myself to an airplane; if it loses air speed, it stalls and falls out of the sky.

My goal entailed starting to live a real life when I reached retirement.

I came within an eyelash of that early retirement goal at fifty-three. However, I will retire as a different person, one with balance in my life. I will resist the temptation of this type-A personality to throw myself into my new business the way I threw myself into my career—honest, I will.

2. Elder Care Lessons Learned

My mother's tragic ordeal took a heavy toll on her as well as on me. Yes, she had dementia, but she made the best of it in a facility that was designed to take care of her medical and physical needs as well as to provide her with a social outlet. And all went well for a while.

I believe that the assisted living facility's medical error precipitated the beginning of the end for my mother. It sent her on a serious downward spiral that accelerated quickly and sent her spinning out of control. I didn't realize the full impact of the medical error at the time. I was not as well-equipped as I thought I would be when I was caught in the eye of the storm.

Key Lessons

Key lessons I would like to share from my elder care experiences are:

- Understand your parent's wishes.
  - ◊ Have all documents in place before you need them.
  - ◊ Understand a living will, DNR, and DNI (Do Not Intubate) orders.
  - ◊ Understand the HIPAA and medical representative rules.
- Get the "facts" from multiple sources.
- Ask good questions over and over.
  - ◊ The nurses know a lot more than you think. Talk to the nurses one on one.
  - ◊ Seek out a care coordinator to help you sort through conflicting information.
  - ◊ Do independent research.
  - ◊ Tell one doctor what the other doctors are saying and evaluate their answers analytically.
    - ☐ The nice doctors aren't necessarily right.
    - ☐ The gruff doctors aren't necessarily wrong.
    - ☐ Members of the medical team might not agree.
  - ◊ Ignoring the facts won't change them.
- Do the best you can with the information you have.
- Use care in making important decisions.
  - ◊ Calmly sort out the options and feelings with your family.
  - ◊ Bring your family in closer, even if it is difficult.
  - ◊ Detach from your emotions to the extent possible.
  - ◊ Find an objective listener to talk to.
  - ◊ Find an objective talker to listen to.
  - ◊ Get help from a friend who cares but is not in grief.

- Exercise extreme caution in other areas of your life.
  - ◊ Realize how vulnerable you really are.
  - ◊ If you are suspicious of any request, order, activity, action, or person, talk to calmer heads immediately.
  - ◊ Don't take anything for granted in times like these.
  - ◊ Ask questions over and over.
  - ◊ Don't make any decisions if you don't have to.
- Interact with your parent in as many ways as you can.
  - ◊ Have fun and make them smile, if possible.
  - ◊ Give them a hug and touch them in other ways.
  - ◊ Enjoy and appreciate the good days.

  Enjoy and appreciate the good days.

  - ◊ Take the bad days in stride.
  - ◊ Observe what is going on around you and them.
- Change your mindset if the decline accelerates.
  - ◊ Observe the trends.
  - ◊ Note that if declines are deeper, rebounds are shallower.
  - ◊ If any care arrangements break down, change them immediately.
- Quality of life is all that matters.
  - ◊ Be realistic when you assess the probabilities and consequences of projected outcomes.
  - ◊ Heroic interventions might hold little long-term promise.
  - ◊ Attack the issue head-on.
  - ◊ Living longer isn't always better.
- Reconnect with your family during and after the loss.
  - ◊ Forgive yourself for any perceived mistakes.
  - ◊ Recognize that you all did the best you could.
  - ◊ Don't look back and play the what-if game.
  - ◊ Be at peace with what is.

◊ Give thanks for the time you had and cherish your memories with your loved one forever.

◊ Plan a commemorative tribute on a special day (birthday, anniversary, Mother's Day, Father's Day).   Nature abhors a vacuum; the pain might resurface unexpectedly if you merely suppress it.

Plan a commemorative tribute on a special day

I had never been responsible for anyone's care before I was responsible for my mother. And I was not a primary caregiver; I filled some patient advocate and care coordinator roles. I went into the situation with my business skills but without any specific knowledge of or experience with the complexities of hospitals and managed care facilities. I did not know the difference between a living will, which I had, and a DNR order, which I did not have.

A complete tangle of requirements exists with HIPAA, power of attorney, authorized medical representative, Medicare limits, supplemental insurance limits, co-pays, and deductibles. The more you know and the sooner that you know it, the better off you will be.

Some facilities will perform heroic end-of-life interventions in order to make money. Others will do them because the family demands them. Other times, one or more doctors think that the interventions will truly help the patient.

Your only defense is to be as informed as possible about who is advocating what intervention and why.

Your only defense is to be as informed as possible about who is advocating what intervention and why. See the elder care quiz at the back of the book.

3. Physical Injury Lessons Learned

"Character—the willingness to accept responsibility for one's own life—is the source from which self-respect springs."
– Joan Didion

My physical injury pulled the rug out from under me. It may have been related to extreme stress from my mother's long-term illness and death in addition my fiancé's predatory and threatening behavior. The other theory is that it was from hunching over a computer for eleven hours a day for decades. Either way, it was a huge setback for me both physically and emotionally.

Before the injury, I skated, played tennis, and was very active. Then I was seriously debilitated with no end in sight. I didn't realize the full impact of the emotional toll that being dependent upon others and that wondering whether I would ever resume normal activities would take on me and my psyche. I was caught unprepared in a storm.

> *I didn't realize the full impact of the emotional toll that being dependent upon others…*

Key Lessons

Key lessons I would like to share from my physical injury experiences if I had to do it all again are:

- Research the injury.
  - ◊ Learn all you can about the injury and the cure.
- Find others with a similar injury.
  - ◊ Chart their recoveries.
  - ◊ Draw similar inferences with your own.
- Find a solid medical team.
  - ◊ Assemble a skilled and caring team that you believe in who can manage your recovery.
  - ◊ Replace those who do not provide either adequate medical or moral support.
- Do something soothing if you must wait.
  - ◊ When I did not have access to a neurologist, I had acupuncture treatments. They helped to settle me and prepare me for my recovery.
  - ◊ Get a massage if you can for touch therapy.
  - ◊ Bring a sense of patience into your recovery.
- Manage the paperwork proactively.
  - ◊ Keep everything up-to-date including medical justification paperwork.

◊   Make co-payments with a credit card so you have permanent receipts if the records are misplaced.

- Understand that recovery takes time.
  - ◊ Tissue repair does not happen overnight.
  - ◊ There are good days, and there are bad days.
  - ◊ There might be setbacks, but keep the faith.
  - ◊ Find hope in the small things until you can see more.
  - ◊ Feel better before you are better.

- Emotional wellbeing supports physical wellbeing.
  - ◊ Emotions are heightened when you are in pain.
  - ◊ Channel emotions toward peaceful endeavors.
  - ◊ Find some time to be at peace each day in a quiet, warm, and safe environment to aid healing.
  - ◊ My fabulous late cat, Katie, was always there for me.

- Do whatever you need to do to get restful sleep, especially in the acute stage in the beginning.
  - ◊ Sleep heals.
  - ◊ Sleep takes your mind off your pain and your troubles.
  - ◊ Have a hot chocolate before bed.

- Realize how vulnerable you are when you are injured.
  - ◊ Only let safe people close to you.
  - ◊ Avoid major life decisions or else seek help.

- Maintain a positive attitude.
  - ◊ It beats the alternative.
  - ◊ It might actually speed your recovery substantially.

- The exercises that you do not like to do probably yield the best results.
  - ◊ Gently test your limits.
  - ◊ Do isometrics as soon and as often as you can.
  - ◊ Push as hard as you can without hurting yourself.

◊ Keep at it; it is so worth it.

◊ Track your progress to keep motivated.

- Thank everyone who helped you to recover.

◊ Most people take their care providers for granted.

◊ Adopt an attitude of sincere gratitude.

I had never experienced such a serious injury, which required ten months to heal. I realize that many others have suffered permanent injuries or injuries far more serious than I could imagine. I do not consider myself an authority on the subject or a particularly difficult case. I can merely relate what happened to me as an individual and outline my recovery process in the hopes of helping others. So it was in that vein that I shared those lessons. See the physical injury quiz at the back of the book.

4. Financial Loss Lessons Learned

"The question isn't at what age I want to retire, it's at what income."
– George Foreman

My financial loss was a major setback to my retirement plans. I have been considered financially savvy most of my life; I have owned ten investment properties and had an excellent career. I spent most of my adult life focused on becoming valued in the marketplace in order to be financially independent.

But when the finish line was in sight, I diverted my attention in an effort to save my relationship. I subsequently lost a fortune and my chance to retire early. In fact, I lost everything that was important to me.

It is ironic that many people criticized me for being totally concentrated on my work and on financial independence. But when my retirement was on the line, I focused on my mother and my fiancé, not on myself. In the end, I will have worked five years longer than I had planned due to my fiancé's dogged interference in the sale of my house.

Key Lessons

Key lessons I would like to share from the experience of my financial loss if I had to do it all again are:

- Keep your eye on the prize.
  - ◊ Focus on the essential steps and timing to reach your goal.
  - ◊ Your net worth can go down a lot faster than it goes up.

    Your net worth can go down a lot faster than it goes up.
  - ◊ Secure your money before you need your money.
  - ◊ If you lose money, don't take on excess risk to make it back.
- Take your profits in a prudent fashion.
  - ◊ Target an exit point for when an asset goes up.
  - ◊ Use stop losses in the markets that have them.
  - ◊ Don't get greedy.
- Look at the problem from as many ways as possible.
- Don't let others influence you if you have a lot more to lose than they do.
- Find a way to get time on your side so your wealth builds more each day.
  - ◊ There are lots of ways to cut your spending.
  - ◊ The best solution might be a hybrid of the options.
  - ◊ Think outside the box: $10,000 annual income replaces $200,000 in capital.
  - ◊ Think long term for all decisions, at least a five-year planning horizon.
  - ◊ See the financial quiz at the back of the book.

5. Relationship Loss Lessons Learned

"The unexamined life is not worth living."
– Socrates

My wedding plans went up in smoke when it seemed that my fiancé expected a $650,000 dowry from me (via a free house)! The so-called love of my life, my alleged soul mate, acted in a vicious, sinister, and predatory manner. But in the end, even after I sold the house, he still wanted to marry me. Go figure!

Key Lessons

Key lessons I would like to share from my relationship loss experience if I had to do it all again are:

- Pick the right person and align your principles, goals, and values.
    - ◊ Test this early in the relationship.
    - ◊ Most people change very little on deeper issues.
    - ◊ Accept "what is" as truth. Will you still go forward?
- Assess the balance in the relationship. How much are you willing to give to the relationship vs. your partner?
    - ◊ Test them with things that you want to do to discern any controlling tendencies and other serious incompatibilities.
    - ◊ It gets harder and harder to walk away over time.
- If you believe your world revolves around one person, begin to diversify.
    - ◊ Get on a path of healing and self-awareness.
    - ◊ Build a support team of positive people.
    - ◊ Build and maintain close connections with friends and family.
- Don't avoid the tough subjects, but rather find a way to discuss them politely when and as they arise.
    - ◊ Discover whether your partner respects your opinion.
    - ◊ If your partner won't talk, what does that tell you?
    - ◊ Don't let tensions build; talk often about how your partner's behavior makes you feel.
    - ◊ Saying "I love you" is easy, but all that counts is action.

- Make major decisions very carefully.
  - ◊ You are only responsible for your actions, not anyone else's.
  - ◊ There is a fifty percent divorce rate, so thousands of suboptimal decisions are made every day.
- Ignore unsolicited advice.
  - ◊ Remember that 20/20 hindsight is one hundred percent accurate.
  - ◊ Ignore people who tell you what you should have done or what you should have known.
- Keep your eye on the prize.
  - ◊ Focus on the most important outcome.
  - ◊ Be fair but firm.

Ignore people who tell you what you should have done or what you should have known.

In addition to these principles, the two quizzes in the back of the book can help you determine if your relationship is healthy and if you're emotionally stable enough to enter a new relationship:

- How to Tell if You are in a Controlling Relationship
- How to Tell if You are Ready for a New Relationship

While reflecting on the key points mentioned above, I realized that I also had the tendency to be somewhat controlling, especially around younger people. On some occasions, I freely offered them my opinions and "sound" advice without being invited to do so. Having realized this aspect of my personality, I sought to curb it and no longer offer unsolicited advice.

6. Emotional Loss Lessons Learned

"Change your thoughts, change your life…"
– Wayne Dyer

My emotional losses utterly devastated me. The total betrayal by my fiancé where our entire relationship hinged on me keeping the house and my retirement plans hinged on me selling the house was mind boggling to say the least. Where could I turn for help?

I know that my losses pale when compared to the losses of others. Most of my losses were mostly reversible. If your loss was more severe than mine, I am truly sorry. If your loss was less severe than mine, I am truly sorry. We all have to deal with our own losses in our own ways. After the carnage, I began a quest to increase my self-awareness and my self-nurturing. I knew I was on my own now—maybe forever.

So I worked on positive thoughts and self-talk. I worked on increasing my empathy and decreasing my judgments of myself and others. Throughout

> *I worked on increasing my empathy and decreasing my judgments of myself and others.*

my life, I had been a very harsh critic of myself; I guess this was a carryover from my parents. The coach training program at IPEC truly changed my life. I have finally learned to accept and love myself unconditionally—a major breakthrough for me. The following list includes individuals who were notable and inspiring contributors to my emotional recovery (many without their knowledge):

- Wayne Dyer, author of *Change Your Thoughts - Change Your Life*
- Bruce Schneider, founder of the IPEC coaching program and author of *Energy Leadership: Transforming Your Workplace and Your Life From the Core*
- Aurora Winter, the Grief Coach and author of *From Heartbreak to Happiness*
- Margaret Paul of InnerBonding.com, author of *Do I Have to Give Up Me to Be Loved By You?*
- Patricia Evans, author of *Controlling People: How to Recognize, Understand, and Deal with People Who Try to Control You*
- Dr. Judith Orloff, author of *Emotional Freedom: Liberate Yourself from Negative Emotions and Transform Your Life*

I thank them for their inspiration and their ability to help others in their times of greatest need.

Key Lessons

Key lessons I would like to share from my emotional loss experience are:

- Change your thoughts.
    - ◊ It makes all the difference in the world.
    - ◊ Value and fully appreciate yourself and your gifts.
    - ◊ It is OK to just "be."
- Tell your story.
    - ◊ The world needs to hear what you have to say.
    - ◊ Opening up is good for you.
    - ◊ It might help someone else.
- Reach out to others.
    - ◊ Find your faith.
    - ◊ Build a support network.
    - ◊ I reached out to three cousins after forty years.
- Give back to the community.
    - ◊ Find an important cause and dive in; it helps you too.
        - □ I give to charity.
        - □ I also give to my church.
    - ◊ When tempted to feel sorry for yourself, look around and count your blessings.
    - ◊ Gratitude is a powerful healing mechanism.
- Filter well-meaning advice very carefully.
    - ◊ Ignore people who blame you; they know not what they speak.
    - ◊ Ignore Monday-morning quarterbacks with 20/20 hindsight vision.
    - ◊ Don't accept anyone else's version of what you should do.
    - ◊ Thank everyone for their input and tell them that you will synthesize it with the inputs of others.

◊ Beware of amateur psychologists; they can do you harm with their trite and misguided musings.

◊ Seek input and advice from multiple sources, but make your own decisions.

◊ Trust but verify the intentions of others.

For your information and amusement, I compiled a list of "21 Stupid Things to Say to Someone Who Has Suffered a Significant Loss"; you can find it at the back of the book.

7. Spiritual Connection Lessons Learned

"Being a spiritual person is synonymous with being a person whose highest priority is to be loving to oneself and others. A spiritual person cares about people… A spiritual person knows that we are all one…"
– Margaret Paul

When I reconnected with God during the darkest days of my mother's illness, I found two things that I was missing in my life: purpose and hope. I discovered in Reverend Jenny Cannon's Disciple Bible study course that I knew the least of anyone in the class, but that meant that I received the most benefit from the study. I took full advantage of the readings and the discussions.

I live my life differently now; each day is a new opportunity to find closer ties to God. Yes, sometimes I revert back to focusing on work deadlines and life's general hustle and bustle, but I get back on track much faster now. Again I have changed my thinking. Now I read a few inspirational emails each morning to start my day.

…each day is a new opportunity to find closer ties to God.

As part of my spiritual journey, which I still consider to be only in the early stages, I now know I have everything that I need to do what I need to do. The key spiritual lessons that I learned are:

• Be aware of God's presence.

• Put God at the center of your life.

- Understand that God is merciful and compassionate.

- Ask for forgiveness and forgive others.

- Read the Bible routinely.

- Express gratitude many times a day.

- Listen for guidance.

- Live compassionately—do unto others as you would have them do unto you.

I know that I will only grow in my faith and understanding as I continue along this path. I suggest that you assess what role your particular style of faith plays in your life along with any recovery aspirations that you might have.

8. Retirement Planning Lessons Learned

"The best way to appreciate your job is to imagine yourself without one."
– Oscar Wilde

At first, I resented the fact that I had to keep working long after my planned retirement. I grumbled all the way into the office, grousing about what I was missing and what I would have been doing if I had been able to retire as planned. If only he hadn't interfered, I wouldn't be stuck still working full time.

But wait a minute, he did interfere, and I did lose a ton of money. I needed this job now more than ever. My job was my primary financial life line for my new future! It was not like I had a choice anymore. So I changed my thinking, now I actually enjoy going to work. I am very grateful that I still have my job.

What a simple thing to do—change your thoughts—in order to change your day. It always sounded rather trite, but it worked for me. Thank you, Wayne Dyer!

I learned that I will only be comfortable in retirement after I've lined up my financial, emotional, and entrepreneurial ducks. I guess I've learned what thousands of other retiree hopefuls have realized: Things change and there's no going back. You had better change with the times or be left behind wondering what happened. Recognize, adapt, and act!

> *You had better change with the times or be left behind wondering what happened.*

Key Lessons

Key lessons that I learned are as follows:

- Assess your emotional readiness for retirement.
    - ◊ What will you do with your time 24/7?
    - ◊ How much of your ego, self image, and feelings of inherent worth are derived from your career?
- Assess your spouse's readiness for this step.
    - ◊ Consider emotional, financial, recreational, and social needs.
    - ◊ Are your dreams aligned?
- Assess your general financial readiness for retirement.
    - ◊ Will you have enough money for your years?
    - ◊ Do a sensitivity analysis on your cash flow projections.
    - ◊ Test your assumptions.
- Estimate your income requirements.
    - ◊ Take your time and run the numbers.
    - ◊ Factor in contingencies.
    - ◊ Factor in inflation and chart the effects.
    - ◊ Consider working longer if you need to.
    - ◊ Start a business if you want to.
- Calculate fixed and variable expenses.
    - ◊ Some things, such as insurance and taxes, cannot be cut.
    - ◊ Factor in inflation and chart the effects.
    - ◊ Consider pre-paying some expenses.
    - ◊ Health care can be a real wild card.
- Everyone begins from a different starting point.
    - ◊ Everyone envisions a different lifestyle and income needs.

◊   Many retirees spend a lot on entertainment in their first five years, then much less after that.

I know that I will only enjoy my retirement after I have saved and planned to the point where I am comfortable. We are all different with diverse plans and varying levels of risk tolerance. See what works for you.

9. Entrepreneurship Lessons Learned

"Every worthwhile accomplishment, big or little, has its stages
of drudgery and triumph; a beginning, a struggle, and a victory."
– Mahatma Gandhi

When I decided to start my own business, I already had a solid foundation in business and problem-solving knowledge and skills, but I had never owned a business before. I learned that unlimited business opportunities are available. The key entrepreneurship lessons I learned are listed in the following:

- Select the right business based on your passion and skills.
- Narrow the focus of the business strategy.
- Develop a detailed business plan.
- Define your unique value proposition.
- Define and provide excellent customer service.
- Define finance requirements and sources of capital.
- Obtain the required training.
- Learn from everyone you meet.
- Network and make connections everywhere.
- Keep scanning the market.
- Revise your plan as needed.
- Execute, test, modify, and execute.
- Outsource non-strategic activities.
- Focus on your strengths and on sales.

- Implement solid systems and tools.

- Conduct two-way interactions with your customers.

- Develop products to meet proven demand.

- Obtain publicity.

- Explore joint-venture opportunities.

I know that as I grow my business, I will encounter many unforeseen challenges and unexpected opportunities, but I am ready. I have everything that I need to succeed. I am doing what I love and I love what I am doing.

CHAPTER 13

Looking Back over It All

*"I like living. I have sometimes been wildly, despairingly,
acutely miserable, racked with sorrow, but through it all, I still
know quite certainly that just to be alive is a grand thing."*
– Agatha Christie

1. What Really Happened

*"We all live with the objective of being happier;
our lives are all different and yet the same."*
– Anne Frank

"Understanding is a two-way street."
– Eleanor Roosevelt

Looking back, I now know that nothing about my relationship was what I thought it was. I tried so hard to save my relationship and my dream. John and I had supported each other through thick and thin. But it appears that the relationship itself was merely an illusion, a complete fraud.

If I had married him, how far would the verbal and emotional abuse and the controlling behaviors have gone? The unintended extra-long engagement provided me with the opportunity to see the real him— unmasked. Thank God.

The good news is that he made his move before we married. He seized his opportunity to take control. His opportunity for economic exploitation occurred when my mother was dying. Her prolonged illness and multiple excruciating ups and downs provided him with tremendous leverage over me.

Ultimately, I lost my life partner and soul mate, but he only lost his pawn. For me, it was a messy breakup and very expensive, but it was almost painless for him. Being with him endangered both my health and my wealth, so it was better for me to go.

I got the message the universe was sending: We were not meant to be. If the house would have sold quickly, I would have married him. If I

Who knows what could have happened to me as his wife?

would have lost less money, I would have married him. If he would have lifted a finger to save our relationship, I would have married him. I was so much in love with him, but now, I thank God that I ended the relationship before a worse fate befell me. Who knows what could have happened to me as his wife? His threats were increasing, and we were only engaged.

I know that in a successful relationship, compromise is required. But not just by one person. In his zeal to punish me, he lost the opportunity to stay in the house that he loved so much. He could have easily bought half. If he had, we would now be together, and under Florida law, he would have some control over me and my money.

Was the whole ordeal solely about control after all—controlling me and my money? Was that power more important than the house itself? Yes, he successfully destroyed our relationship and sabotaged my retirement plans. Was the house merely the battleground for ultimate control?

When we finally broke up, amazingly, he still wanted to marry me. Looking back, I have lived a rags to riches story. My unwavering goal was success. Well, as it turns out, I achieved so much success that I ended up with a successful businessman who wanted to marry me for my money. So I guess the universe handed me what I was seeking. I guess that after I had been thoroughly punished for my disobedience, he was willing to give me another chance to please him and to do everything his way as long as he had access to my money. Maybe he thought that I had been trained by his threats and his punishments even though all of his threats turned out to be hollow.

At the end, he actually talked about moving out of his beloved neighborhood. *What?* I wondered. *He destroyed my life because he could never, ever be happy anywhere other than the paradise where he demanded to live, and now he is casually thinking about moving away from the neighborhood of his dreams. What? What? What?*

Up until the very end, he would admit nothing. Alas, truth only came in five-minute increments with John. Truth must be painful for him because it faded very quickly, and selfishness and deceit always quickly re-emerged in full force. Comically but sadly, he blamed our breakup on me talking with coaches in my professional coaching program. To him, his five threats did not seem to be major contributing factors—neither did high-jacking my house or sabotaging my retirement plans. This must be what Teflon looks like in the flesh: Not even a small portion of responsibility would stick to him; he purposely slipped off the blame with one of his slick, never-ending excuses. Consequently, he placed the blame for our failed relationship squarely on me talking with coaches. He thought he could do or say anything without any accountability or concern for downstream impacts.

> *Truth must be painful for him…*

He searched for something—anything outside of himself—to blame. But the answer to the demise of our twenty-one-year relationship was much closer; he only needed to look into a mirror.

> *…he only needed to look into a mirror.*

On his way out, he asked that I please not contact any member of his family. I guess that he did not want them to discover the truth about his actions. Surely his parents had raised him much better than that. Is it possible that he actually felt ashamed about how he treated me and the carnage that he caused? He also told me he would tell everyone that our decision to split was mutual and that I specifically requested that none of them contact me. I viewed it as just another confabulation, twisting the facts to suit his purposes.

2. The Takeaway Messages

"To live is the rarest thing in the world. Most people exist, that is all."
– Oscar Wilde

- I planned to start living when I retired; I never got the chance.

- I planned to spend more time with my extended family when I retired; I never got the chance.

- I planned to reach out and make a whole host of new friends when I retired; I never got the chance.

- I planned to put more balance in my life when I retired; I never got the chance.

- I planned to get more involved in my new church and new community when I retired; I never got the chance.

Living in the future is no way to live at all! I believed that financial independence would "save" me, but that is not the way to live. Living in the future is no way to live at all! The only time truly available to us is the present—now. There are no guarantees in life, and no one has promised you tomorrow. So what can you do today?

You might wonder how my mother's terminal illness, my planned retirement date, the housing crash, and a debilitating physical injury all happened within months of each other. What had I done to upset the universe? What were the fates telling me with this series of tragic coincidences?

Yes, I know that stuff happens and sometimes happens in bunches. And when serious stuff happens, it is a supreme test of your principles, values, resilience, and faith. Maybe I had more than my share at a single point in time. Life is full of challenges, but many others have faced and conquered far greater ordeals. Many have suffered greater or more traumatic losses. I am not remarkable, I am an everyday person. My trial may be different from others, but many amazing recovery stories occur all around you.

Lessons for Life

The lessons we can all take away are many. We can choose to:

- Live a life of gratitude.

- Build foundations in faith and in hope.

- Be careful what we wish for.

- Assemble connections with family, friends, and community.
- Construct emotional resilience to smooth over the bumps.
- Forgive others and ask for forgiveness.
- Start each day with the goal to help others.

Trials test not only you but also those around you. As you chart your course, it is important for you to begin to identify:

- Who will step up when the going gets tough?
- Who will stand by you?
- Who will go the extra mile for you?

Perhaps we can only see the true character of those around us in times of trials and trouble. In parallel, it is important for you to consider your true character. Surely, we can see our own true character in times of trouble.

- Will you step up when the going gets tough?
- Will you stand by those who depend on you?
- Will you go the extra mile?
- Will you like what you see in yourself?

CHAPTER 14

Tools to Clear the Path to Recovery

"Being free means surviving rejections, major and minor,
without turning on yourself or allowing them to define you."
– Dr. Judith Orloff

Up until this point, this book has focused on my trials and tribulations and my eventual recovery. If you or someone you know is suffering from a significant loss, the next sections of this book focus on helping others to recover from their losses. Perhaps the loss was financial from the real estate crash or the stock market tumble, or the damage could be emotional from a devastating relationship breakup or the excruciating complexity of coping with elder care issues. Whatever the situation, when these things happen, they test your ability to cope and move on with your life. But now is the time for recovery! Are you ready? Are you really ready?

1. Your Values Are the Key Foundation

"Don't wait for a crisis to discover what is important in your life."
– Anonymous

"I experienced that familiar 'deer in the headlights' paralysis knowing that
my values were on the line and that either decision had real consequences."
– Doug Silsbee

Your values play an important part in defining your character, and they'll play a major role in any recovery process. If you're to truly live out your values going forward, it is important for you to define these principles with specificity in the different roles that you play in your life.

You can make a different list of values for each of your different roles. Some people prefer to do this for three roles for themselves, and they also think about values they are looking for in a current or future mate. The common sample roles are:

- Self,
- Family,
- Job or career,
- Spouse, Significant Other, Partner or
- Other.

There is no limit to the number of roles for which you can define your values.

Principles that you believe are essential to you as a person, as a citizen of the world, might constitute one list focusing, for example, on discovery. In your role as part of your family, other values such as harmony might be more important in that context. Then when you think about your role in your career or job, different values such as professionalism might emerge as more important.

Key Steps in the Values Exercise

- First, select a role with which to begin.
- Review the values presented here and add others if needed.
- Make a list of the significant values that resonate with you in that particular role.
- If you prefer, you can complete this important values exercise in the 5Es workbook specifically designed for this program at http://www. BouncingBackFromLoss.com/5EsWorkbook. This is especially helpful if you'd like to do the values exercise for multiple roles.

- When your list is complete, go back over it and circle the essential, fundamental top four to five values. These are your core values for that role.

It's not as easy as it sounds. Building the list is inclusive and expansive; culling it to the top four to five values takes deep thought, tough choices, and prioritization. Be mindful that you are not rejecting the other values. They are still your values, but you are merely labeling them as second-tier values, for now.

Look at each of your top four to five values in the context of your selected role and write a few sentences about each one, highlighting the following:

- Why did you select it?
- Why is it important to you?
- Does this value relate to other values on your priority list?
- What does it mean to you if you successfully embody that value?
- Are you fully living that value now or is there work to be done?

After you fully explore the top values for one role, think about what these values mean for your life in the future. Are you committed to making changes—large or small—based on these values? Why?

Then if you choose, go back and do the same exercise for your other roles. You may find it interesting to see the similarities and differences between the personal and professional values lists and the personal and family lists. Possible values are listed below:

Acceptance	Awe	Cheerfulness
Accommodation	Balance	Clarity
Accomplishment	Beauty	Commitment
Accountability	Belonging	Communication
Achievement	Boldness	Community
Adaptability	Bravery	Compassion
Adventure	Calmness	Compromise
Appreciation	Character	Concern
Awareness	Charity	Confidence

Connection	Goodwill	Pleasure
Consciousness	Gratitude	Practicality
Conservation	Happiness	Principles
Consideration	Harmony	Professionalism
Cooperation	Health	Punctuality
Courage	Honesty	Quality
Courtesy	Honor	Reasonableness
Creativity	Humility	Recognition
Credibility	Humor	Reconciliation
Curiosity	Imagination	Resilience
Decisiveness	Independence	Respect
Dependability	Insight	Restraint
Determination	Integrity	Romance
Discipline	Intimacy	Security
Effectiveness	Intuition	Self-control
Efficiency	Joy	Selflessness
Empathy	Justice	Self-reliance
Encouragement	Kindness	Sensitivity
Enjoyment	Kinship	Sincerity
Enthusiasm	Leadership	Spirituality
Equality	Love	Sportsmanship
Environment	Loyalty	Stability
Excellence	Mindfulness	Teaching
Family	Mentoring	Tolerance
Fairness	Motivation	Trust
Faith	Natural living	Truth
Fidelity	Openness	Understanding
Flexibility	Optimism	Virtue
Freedom	Passion	Vision
Friendship	Peace	Warmth
Fulfillment	Perseverance	Winning
Fun	Persistence	Wisdom
Generosity	Personal growth	Other _____
Giving	Playfulness	Other _____

2. Overview of the 5 Es to Recovery

*"You yourself, as much as anybody in the
entire universe, deserve your love and affection."*
– Buddha

"Don't believe everything you think."
– Marci Shimoff

Recovery can be fast or it can be slow. Make no mistake—recovery is not a point in time; it is indeed a process. Healing is not marked by a singular point in time when one day you are down and then the next you are "recovered" from your loss. That is not the way it works.

If you seem to be stuck, rest assured that you are not alone. Many face their trials without the tools that they need. A more caring, compassionate approach is required. Importantly, remember that everyone:

- is diverse to begin with,

- is starting from a different point,

- has experienced a unique loss,

- will move through the loss at his/her own pace, and

- will end up at a different place.

Whatever your loss, be assured the stress takes a heavy toll on you, whether you are aware of it or not. Stress can affect you in many different forms; it can make you irritable, sleepless, or gain weight, but it is pure toxic stress, nonetheless. The adverse physical impacts of stress have been widely documented and are not to be underestimated. It is critical to adopt tools and practices to insulate yourself from the harmful effects of long-term stress. No benefit whatsoever is gained from constant worrying, being uptight, and internalizing constant stress. It does no good, and it does indeed do harm.

...stress takes a heavy toll on you...

Through my extensive research involving scores of books, hundreds of articles, dozens of teleclasses on healing and coping, my two coach training programs, and my own personal experience, I discovered five key steps that clear the path to recovery.

I've named them the 5 Es to Recovery, and with them, I have designed a groundbreaking recovery program that I would like to share with you. I hope that the 5 Es will accelerate your healing and recovery. If your healing has been slow so far, the 5 Es to Recovery can help you:

- shortcut your recovery and begin the healing,
- put the past behind you once and for all,
- release your anger and resentment,
- embrace the loss and move forward,
- build networks to provide you with continued support,
- handle what life throws at you next, and
- help you plan a new and brighter future.

FIVE Es TO RECOVERY

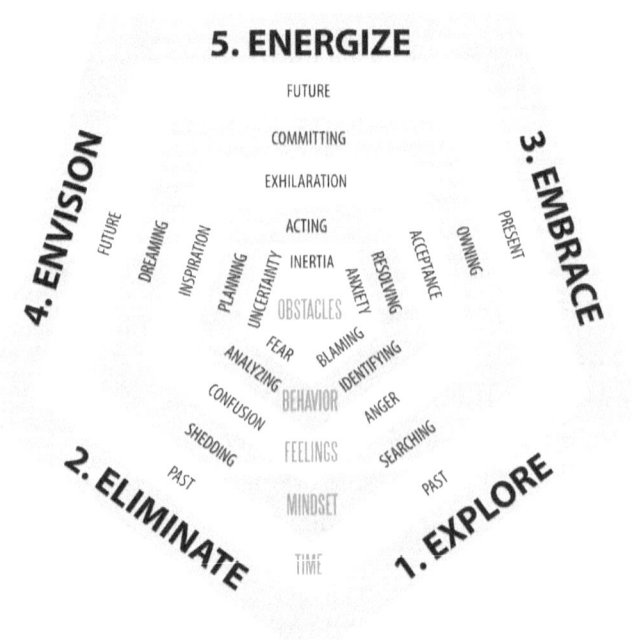

The 5 Es to Recovery might just be the answer that you've been seeking. If you've tried to recover from a single loss or multiple losses on your own and it is taking far longer than you expected or you just don't think that you have everything you need, then this is an exciting time in your recovery process. You picked up this book for a reason; you have indeed come to the right place. It is time to breathe a sigh of relief; the time to heal is now! If you experience the following feelings, it is time to attack them head on:

- Sadness
- Loss
- Vulnerability
- Low self-esteem
- Doubt
- Fear
- Worry
- Anger
- Guilt
- Resentment
- Decreased energy
- Decreased willingness to try new things
- Increased irritability
- Sleeping either too little or too much
- Eating either too little or too much

The 5 Es to Recovery provide you with a step-by-step process that lays out building blocks and provides a foundation for you to build upon in your own personal recovery journey. The 5 Es are:

1. Explore what happened.
2. Eliminate the unwanted feelings.
3. Embrace the situation.
4. Envision a new future.
5. Energize your world.

Today is a new day; your recovery begins now! This powerful process will help you accept what is and move on to create a new and vibrant life. The next five sections in this chapter explore each of the 5 Es in turn.

3. The First E: Explore What Happened

"Learn from yesterday, live for today, hope for tomorrow."
– Albert Einstein

Let's review the first E: explore what happened. In order to achieve a full recovery, it is important to place all of the facts and feelings out on the table. The first E encompasses seven actions. If you have suffered multiple losses, you have the option of processing them one at a time. Or if the losses are inter-related, you can process them at the same time. The most important determinant is how you think about your losses.

In order to achieve a full recovery, it is important to place all of the facts and feelings out on the table.

First, find a notebook to collect your thoughts and track your progress. Or if you would find it easier and more convenient, you can use the *5Es to Recovery Workbook,* specifically designed for the 5Es program that is presented in this book with input sheets that can be printed again and again. Go to http://www.BouncingBackFromLoss.com/5EsWorkbook to pick up your own copy of the 5Es Workbook.

Action 1: Write Down What Happened to You in Your Loss

Start to write down what happened from the beginning to the end; do this until you have it all out. I ask that you please put down this book now and write at least three paragraphs about what you went through, addressing the major details of your loss. If you have more to write, just keep on going.

If you choose not to do this step now but to keep on reading, remember to come back when you are committed to beginning your recovery in earnest. Recovery takes both commitment and action. The improvement you can expect is directly proportional to your levels of commitment and action. I strongly encourage you to write about your loss now.

I was very skeptical of this action at first. I never kept a diary or a journal when I was little. Growing up with two older brothers, it would have been impossible for me to keep it safe or secret. But somehow I convinced myself to do this step. I attribute that to a teleclass given by Aurora Winter, the Grief Coach. I took her teleclass in the middle of my professional coach training program, and for some reason, I was more receptive then to the message than the other times I had heard it. At the time, I did not even realize that I was experiencing "grief"; I thought I was experiencing "loss."

Anyway, thanks to Aurora, I pushed myself to write my story. Surprisingly, I was very relieved to get the facts down on paper. They had been circling around and around in my head. After they were on paper, my brain was free to sort out the next steps and move forward. It felt great to find a step that actually helped me. No one was more skeptical than I was that this activity would actually accomplish anything. Thankfully, I found clarity.

As it turns out, writing down what happened was a very powerful tool; it focused my attention and freed my mind for other things. It is similar to creating a to-do or shopping list. After an item is written on the list, you don't have to think about it anymore; you know that it is taken care of.

> *...writing down what happened was a very powerful tool; it focused my attention and freed my mind for other things.*

When I wrote down what happened to me, I began to make progress in my recovery where before I had been stuck. At least a new set of thoughts started turning around in my head—not just the same old tired ones.

About the time that I finished writing my story, I received an email from the *Wake Up Your Life* series of books. They had a new book in the works featuring "Bouncing Back" stories. *How appropriate,* I thought. I expanded my brief story to include my recovery process and outcomes, and it was accepted for publication. My mini-story is presented in the best-selling anthology *Bouncing Back – Thriving in Changing Times* with Wayne Dyer, John Assaraf, Brian Tracy, and David Riklan. I found it a privilege to be included with these esteemed authors; the stories are nothing short of remarkable.

When you decide to put your story down on paper, you certainly do not need to publish it—you don't even need to show it to anyone else, but you can if you wish. The point is that you will gain a psychological benefit from writing your story down. I can personally attest to this.

Action 2: Assess Your Key Feelings About Your Losses

After you've written what happened to you, Action 2 will focus on the feelings surrounding your losses. Start with a deep breath and quiet your mind; just sit in silence, in peace, for a few moments. Then summon your feelings associated with the loss.

When you think about your trial, what feelings come to mind? There could be a blizzard of emotions surrounding your loss. This step involves searching

There could be a blizzard of emotions surrounding your loss.

and seeking. A list of emotions is provided for you to circle or to write in your notebook or 5Es workbook. Circle or list all of the emotions that you feel; we will go back later to sort them out. Do you now feel:

- all alone
- guilty
- trapped
- unlovable
- hopeless
- stuck
- unworthy
- defeated
- powerless
- victimized
- helpless
- desperate
- nervous
- like you're going in circles
- fearful
- unfulfilled
- confused
- vengeful

- vindictive
- lost
- defeated
- abandoned
- numb
- the need to suppress your feelings
- doubtful
- that everyone expects you to be better by now
- barely there
- disappointed
- relieved to be getting better
- acceptance
- harmony
- appreciative

- gratitude
- like you've turned the corner
- like you're hitting your stride
- almost there
- understanding
- the need to share
- like reaching out to help others
- like giving back
- peace
- lovable
- tolerant
- non-judgmental
- satisfied
- joyful
- fulfilled

- angry
- bitter
- ashamed
- sad
- apologetic
- lonely
- furious

- jealous
- enraged
- betrayed
- in denial
- judgmental
- defensive
- threatened

- withdrawn
- anxious
- hurt
- incredulous
- in despair
- untrusting
- insecure

Are there any other major emotions that you are feeling that are not on the list? Add them to your notebook and please send them to me at BouncingBackNow@comcast.net.

Action 3: Prioritize Your Three Top Feelings

Select the top three feelings from Action 2 based on the feeling's intensity and write them down here or in your notebook.

1. _____

2. _____

3. _____

These three emotions hold the key to your recovery because this is where your energy is focused now.

Action 4: Elaborate on Your Three Top Feelings

Document the key reasons associated with the strong feelings surrounding your loss. Now explore each of these feelings, and then describe them in more detail:

I feel (emotion 1) because _____.
I feel (emotion 2) because _____.
I feel (emotion 3) because _____.

This exercise might have exhausted some of your strongest unresolved feelings. If not, go to your notebook and keep on writing until you feel that your emotions and the associated rationale for each emotion have been fully explored. You can perform your custom recovery process in the privacy of your own home on your schedule.

You are now fully in control of your recovery. You are now fully in control of your recovery. Take whatever time you need and take the steps you need to take to make this work for you. Feel free to add more emotions to the list and to add more reasons. Gather that energy and let it out.

Action 5: Complete the Statement

As you begin to identify, document, and resolve your feelings, I would like you to complete the following statement:

If I could only conquer my feeling of _____, then I'd be well on my way to recovery. This feeling of _____ really holds me back. Up until now, I have been unable to get past it.

When you read the completed statement, how does it make you feel? Write down your reaction in your notebook. This is where you are today, where you are stuck now. But rest assured, that is about to change soon.

Now let's move on to the next action under the first E—to assess your support system. This important step establishes the sources of support that are available to you and the quality of support that they can provide.

Action 6: Assess Your Support System

"A lot of kneeling will keep you in good standing."
– Christian prayer

Possessing high-quality support is very important to your recovery process. In this action, we analyze the sources and the strength of your support system. Draw a checkmark (or write Y for yes and N for no) where you have support.

Possessing high-quality support is very important to your recovery process.

	Y/N	Strength 1-10
• Self	_____	_____
• Spouse/partner	_____	_____
• Siblings	_____	_____
• Children	_____	_____
• Parents	_____	_____
• Close friends	_____	_____
• Church	_____	_____
• Coach	_____	_____
• Counselor	_____	_____
• Other _____	_____	_____
• Other _____	_____	_____

For those items marked yes, please rate the strength of that support on a scale of 1-10 with 10 being the highest level of support. This rating is best based on how you feel at the end of an interaction with that person. If the person is compassionate and non-judgmental and makes you feel better, they would receive a higher rating, for example, than an impatient individual who sometimes makes you feel sad or guilty.

Take a moment and review your list. Were you surprised by any of your answers in this step? What are your answers telling you? What actions, if any, do you need to take based on these findings? Do you need to add others to your support system? Why?

Action 7: How Your Support System Can Empower You

After your support system is in place, you know where to turn for help. And sometimes you will find that the answer lies inside of you. In this step, please list three specific ways that you will work with your support system over the next week.

1. _____

2. _____

3. _____

This action plan will help keep you focused. Now that you've completed the first E in the 5 Es to Recovery, take a few minutes to write in your notebook the impact that this work has had on you and note your reactions to your feelings. Are there any important observations that you'd like to document at this stage? After completing these seven actions in this first E, you are ready to progress to the second E: eliminate unwanted feelings.

4. The Second E: Eliminate Unwanted Feelings

"No one can insult you or hurt your feelings without your permission..."
– Eleanor Roosevelt

Let's review the second E: eliminate unwanted feelings. There are eight actions in the second E. Some of the major emotional offenders can be summarized in the acronym: FRUGAL, which is composed of six major feelings.

- Fear
- Resentment
- Unhappiness
- Guilt
- Anger
- Loneliness

The feeling of fear includes an element of doubt and worry. Up until this point, these emotions might have served you well. It is very natural to experience these emotions in times of pain and loss. They may provide you with comfort and a sense of the familiar. These emotions form an essential part of the healing process. But there comes a point when these emotions no longer serve you; in fact they hold you back. At that point, you can begin your journey to recovery in earnest.

But there comes a point when these emotions no longer serve you; in fact they hold you back.

You are ready to conquer the feelings in FRUGAL! More than many other emotions, an excess of these feelings can tremendously damage and hamper your recovery. In order to achieve a full recovery, it is important to remove these powerful weights from your psyche.

These feelings can keep you stuck where you are and hinder your recovery. So start to write down which of these six feelings you have and explain why you have them. Sort through them and get to the bottom of this to help clear the way to your recovery. Write about three paragraphs in your notebook, elaborating on these feelings and how they affect you. If you have more to write, just keep on writing.

> *These feelings can keep you stuck where you are and hinder your recovery.*

Action 1: Write Down Why You Feel FRUGAL

This will give you an understanding of your feelings and how they relate to each other and your current state of mind.

I feel _____ because _____.

I feel _____ because _____.

I feel _____ because _____.

Action 2: Assess the Benefits of these Feelings

"Your attitude is an expression of your values, beliefs and expectations."
– Brian Tracy

Now that you've identified the sources of your feelings, to what extent do you believe each emotion serves you? On a scale of 1-10 (with 1 meaning "no, definitely not helpful" and 10 meaning "yes, definitely helpful"), rate the extent to which you believe each feeling facilitates your recovery.

Scale of 1-10

- Fear   _____
- Resentment   _____
- Unhappiness   _____
- Guilt   _____

- <u>A</u>nger _____
- <u>L</u>oneliness _____

These feelings might provide you with comfort, a makeshift shield against the world. Begin to list why these feelings benefit you and what it *You are now officially in charge of your feeling replacement team!* might take to begin to release them from your life. Often it is a good idea to substitute other feelings for FRUGAL. Nature abhors a vacuum; these feelings need to be replaced with other emotions. For example, replace fear with hope, or anger with tolerance. Review the list of emotions presented in action two of the first E if you'd like. You are now officially in charge of your feeling replacement team!

Action 3: Assess the Costs of These Feelings

Now that you identified the benefits of these feelings, to what extent do you believe each emotion harms you? To what extent do these feelings keep you stuck? On a scale of 1-10 (with 10 meaning "yes, definitely harmful" and 1 meaning "no, definitely not harmful"), rate the extent to which you believe each feeling harms or hinders your recovery.

Scale of 1-10

- <u>F</u>ear _____
- <u>R</u>esentment _____
- <u>U</u>nhappiness _____
- <u>G</u>uilt _____
- <u>A</u>nger _____
- <u>L</u>oneliness _____

These feelings unfairly rob you of your "now." Change the way you think about this, and you will change every part of your life. You have the power to shake off and replace these emotions.

Many of us do not consciously realize that the only time available to us is the present or NOW. You may often dwell on the past or worry about the future. In the meantime, your life passes you by. Minutes simply go down the drain—right in front of you. You may see it to some extent; yet somehow, you still don't truly see it. That introduces an interesting question: What time is truly at your disposal? In fact, the only time you can do something is the present—NOW. Each minute of your life is perishable. So use it or lose it.

> *Each minute of your life is perishable. So use it or lose it.*

Action 4: Choose How You Feel

"The only problem with leaving and going someplace else is that you take yourself with you." – Esther Hicks

Select an emotion, any emotion. Now bring it into reality. Example: *I choose to feel <u>sad</u> for the next twenty seconds.*

I choose to feel _____ for the next twenty seconds.

Now do it. This step illustrates the extent of power you have over your feelings. I'd like you to work on a second exercise with me now. Please imagine yourself in your car on a crowded street. The red traffic light seems to be excessively long. Running just a tad bit late, you're ready to get moving. You notice the cars around you—particularly a red one beside you. Just as the light turns green, the driver in the red car speeds up and cuts in front of you. Then before he has the chance to fully merge into your lane, he stops unexpectedly. What the heck is he doing? Based on this scenario, survey your mind and body.

- How do you feel about this? Did you get angry?
- What are you saying to yourself?
- What are your prevailing thoughts?
- What reactions do you notice in your body?
- Is there tension? Changes in your posture, jaw, or hands? Elevated heart rate? Other noticeable effects?

Physiological changes in your body can be induced by powerful thoughts and feelings. Step back and notice the incredible power of your imagination. In reality, nothing happened to you. Hopefully you still are reading this book, but your body has reacted as if the situation were real. It is like crying at the movies: We know that it's not real, but we still find that we are emotionally invested anyway.

For the third exercise, imagine that you are leaving an outdoor café on a pleasant afternoon in late spring. You just had a nice time catching up with your friends. It is one of your favorite cafés, and you feel welcome there. Take your time to visualize this. High in the bright blue sky, the sun radiates a wonderful feeling of warmth. You stand at the corner preparing to cross the street when someone runs up and taps you on the shoulder to return your wallet that you forgot on the table in the café.

- How do you feel about this? Are you surprised, perhaps thankful?

- What are you saying to yourself?

- What are your prevailing thoughts?

- What reactions do you notice in your body?

- Is there a sigh of relief? A release of tension in your jaw and shoulders? Other noticeable effects?

Now neither of these incidents actually happened to you. But you chose to feel these emotions and make them real with a mere suggestion. You can do this same thing every minute of the day. You have the power. Yes, you really do. You alone hold the key to your feelings. You have just proven to yourself in the last three exercises that you can make yourself agitated or calm. Isn't that an amazing power? Well, it is yours—at your disposal. And you have had this power all along. But now you know you have it, you own it, and you can use it at will.

You alone hold the key to your feelings.

Take this opportunity to make the commitment to yourself to:

- Choose how you feel, and

- Choose how you react.

You demonstrated to yourself that how you feel is really your choice. Harness this awesome power in your life.

Action 5: Choose How Long You Will Have These Feelings

"The greater the difficulty, the more glory in surmounting it."
– Epicurus

This action is designed to help you see what the status quo costs you. These feelings cause you some good or you would not keep them around. Perhaps the feeling makes you feel safe and protected or provides you with some other valuable benefit. How long have you had them? Only you can answer that, but for this exercise, let's use one month as our baseline. Over the past month, how many hours have you spent feeling:

Hours

- Fear   _____

- Resentment   _____

- Unhappiness   _____

- Guilt   _____

- Anger   _____

- Loneliness   _____

How many hours does that add up to? _____ hours

If you've experienced these feelings longer than one month, let's assume that your feelings are in a steady state. Use the number of hours that you felt this way in one month to discover how many hours you've felt this way in total by multiplying the total hours you've felt this way for the past month by the number of months that you've experienced this emotion:

Example: *3 months = 3 x 12 hours = 36 hours total*

Yours: _ months = _ x _____ hours = _____

The next time you say that you don't have time to exercise, play with your kids, or get a manicure, think about all of those hours you've spent going nowhere with these feelings. Round and round. Over and over.

The next step is to decide how much longer you will choose to hold on to these feelings. Over the next month, how many hours will you spend feeling:

Hours

- <u>F</u>ear   _____

- <u>R</u>esentment   _____

- <u>U</u>nhappiness   _____

- <u>G</u>uilt   _____

- <u>A</u>nger   _____

- <u>L</u>oneliness   _____

Please complete the following statement:

I will hold on to my feelings for (how long) _____. Then, I will banish them!

It is your choice how long you decide to hold on to your feelings, so please choose carefully and wisely. As a highly individualized exercise, you might decide to banish them immediately. You may decide to spend just one more week with your feelings of loss. Pick a date or an event after which you will no longer harbor these feelings. Then routinely banish them when they raise their pesky heads.

Alternatively, you might decide to spend a few more weeks with your feelings of loss. If that is what you choose and what you will stick to, then fine. But please do not wallow in your feelings. Accept them, honor them, thank them, and then banish them. You no longer need them. Really, you don't! Your new life is waiting for you just around the corner.

Do this exercise thoughtfully now, and believe me, you will not regret it. Changing any thoughts and behaviors that we think serve us in some way involves hard work. I created an abstract equation to depict the impetus to change and the resistance to change:

$$L = D + C - S - F$$

L = Likelihood of change

D = Dissatisfaction with the status quo

C = Commitment to action

S = Satisfaction with the status quo

F = Fear of change

In other words, change more likely occurs where high levels of dissatisfaction with the status quo and high levels of commitment to action exist. Change less likely occurs where high levels of attachment and satisfaction with the status quo and high levels of resistance or fear of change exist. You will change when you are sick and tired of being where you are. So why wait? The slogan for my company is Just Say No To The Status Quo™, and I live this out. You can too!

Action 7: Chart Your Recovery Progress Line

> *"Happiness…is not a destination: it is a manner of traveling."*
> – Haim Ginott

All of these feelings have carried you to where you are now. Stop and celebrate for a moment—congratulations on your progress so far! Let's chart your progress on a recovery line.

- Place an "S" on the recovery line for where you started.
- Place an "N" on the recovery line for where you are now.
- Place an "M" on the recovery line for where you want to be in one month.

Please be honest. Chart your first reaction and don't over-think it.

Loss <---> Recovery

How willing are you to step out of the pattern you are in?

> *"Insanity is doing the same things over and over*
> *and expecting a different result."*
> – Albert Einstein

Action 8: Identify What You Are Missing with These Feelings

In many cases, our feelings keep us trapped in places that are suboptimal. Your life may pass you by, but where are you?

Break through the chains of the past... Are you a spectator standing on the sidelines of your own life due to these feelings? How great would it be to eradicate them once and for all?

Break through the chains of the past: the hurts, the slights, the injuries, the pain—let them all go. You no longer need these feelings to protect you.

> *"Man cannot discover new oceans unless he*
> *has the courage to lose sight of the shore."*
> – Andre Gide

List five major things that you miss out on because of these feelings. These areas can be personal, financial, career related, relational, recreational, or any area of your life.

Example: *When I feel sad, then I don't go out dancing with my friends.*

- When I feel _____, then I don't_____.
- When I feel _____, then I don't_____.
- When I feel _____, then I don't_____.
- When I feel _____, then I don't _____.
- When I feel _____, then I don't _____.

If you need more time, take it. Sort this out now. Put the book down and work on it or schedule a time when you can commit to doing this exercise with your full attention. Your recovery depends upon it. Often we need to remind ourselves what we miss by maintaining the status quo.

Often we need to remind ourselves what we miss by maintaining the status quo.

At times, you'll need to be so dissatisfied with the current situation that you'll willingly take the risks that moving on entails. Now that you are fully in charge, filter the stimuli of the world around you; don't let the bad stuff in. You are one hundred percent responsible for your own emotions. Be aware of your own buttons. Learn to put a circuit breaker in place. Work on yourself. Insulate yourself from the cacophony of daily life and focus on your feelings—you can relax, meditate, or simply daydream. At first, you might find it uncomfortable to take this time out for yourself, but it will build up your resilience to face new challenges. I am offering my readers a free teleseminar on the second E, Eliminate the Unlimited Feelings, to help you navigate this very important step. Sign up at http://www.BouncingBackFromLoss.com/seminar.

"If you let go, you will grow."
– Leslie Vernick

5. The Third E: Embrace the Situation

"When you lose, don't lose the lesson."
– Dalai Lama

This third E—embrace the situation—naturally builds on the first two Es. In the third E, with nine actions, we accept what is. We accept that:

- what happened really happened,

- no amount of wishing and hoping can change what occurred,

- we still might not understand why it transpired,

- we might not like it, and

- it did take place.

That is the starting point for your new future. There is no going back; you can only move forward. The past is the past; it is gone and of no use to you now whatsoever. You live in the now, and your dreams are in the future. What you can change is your now and your future; remember the serenity prayer:

"God grant me the serenity to accept the things I cannot change, the courage to change the things I can, and the wisdom to know the difference. Living one day at a time, enjoying one moment at a time, and accepting hardships as the pathway to peace…"
– Reinhold Niebuhr

Action 1: What Happened Really Happened

Let's look at individual phrases in the serenity prayer. Write down answers in your notebook for each question below.

1. What do you need to accept?
2. What can you change?
3. Do you know the difference?
4. How do you know the difference?
5. Are you living one day at a time?
6. Are you enjoying one moment at a time?
7. Are you accepting hardships as a part of life?

"Coming to terms with the parts of a change that you cannot control is critical to being successful…let them go."
– Chris Clarke-Epstein

Action 2: Tell Your Story to an Empathetic Listener—You

As it turns out, most of us are much harder on ourselves than we are on other people. Some of us find it difficult to extend empathy to ourselves. So in this action, you will listen to your story as if it were being told by a friend so that you can demonstrate empathy for the storyteller. You can be your own advocate and best friend. Imagine that a close friend tells you a story about a significant loss; imagine that your story has now become your friend's tale.

Pretend that what happened to you really happened to your friend. Listen as "your friend" recites the account. Get in character (as your friend) as he/she tells you this powerful story of loss aloud. Truly delve into the emotions of the story. How does it make you feel to hear this painful story?

- What are your reactions to your friend's story?
- What are your emotions?
- Do you empathize with the storyteller?
- Do you feel tolerance or compassion?
- Do you want to reach out and try to help the storyteller?
- Do you give them a break for doing what they thought was best at the time, given the available information?
- Do you think that they could have done more?
- Do you judge them on the outcome now that all the facts are in?

Note your feelings and reactions in your notebook.

Action 3: Assess Your Reaction to the Story

In this step, I'd like you to assess your friend's story and your friend's actions.

- Did any of your reactions to the story surprise you?
- Were you harder on your friend or on yourself (even though the situation was the same)?
- What other insights did you notice?
- Overall, how did you react to the story told by your friend?

Note your feelings and reactions in your notebook.

Action 4: Forgive the Storyteller

> *"How far that little candle throws his beams!*
> *So shines a good deed in a weary world."*
> – William Shakespeare

Take steps to forgive the storyteller. After listening carefully to the tale of loss, decide right now that you will indeed forgive the storyteller. In your notebook, write these words three times:

- I forgive the storyteller (myself) for my role in the loss.
- I forgive myself for my role in the loss.
- I forgive myself for my role in the loss.

Now read them back aloud, becoming louder and more forceful with each line until finally you shout, **"I forgive myself for my role in the loss!"** You can repeat this as many times as you like to get the energy out. You need to own your feelings before you can release them. Then forgive yourself and release the negative feelings and energy.

Action 5: Letting Go of the Other Feelings

On a scale of 1-10 (with 10 being the highest), rate the following questions here or in your notebook:

To what extent have you forgiven yourself for
your role in the loss?   _____

To what extent have you forgiven others
involved in your loss?   _____

To what extent do you harbor resentment
regarding your loss?   _____

To what extent do you blame others for your loss?   _____

To what extent are you angry over your loss?   _____

Analyze your answers and explore why you answered the way you did.

Action 6: Learn to Deal with Well-Intentioned Fools

No one says that what has happened to you is what is best for you. Well, I take that back. Some well-meaning but clumsy amateur psychologists might tell you that what occurred is "all for the best." Most people suffering from a serious loss are not ready to hear foolish statements like that.

Some well-meaning but unskilled people might even tell you that you asked for your loss. While others might say that you attracted it and caused your loss yourself. People are at the ready to tell you exactly what you should do next, but

> *Some well-meaning but unskilled people might even tell you that you asked for your loss.*

beware. I compiled a list of "21 Stupid Things to Say to People When They Have Faced a Loss" in the back of the book.

These statements do not help. Ignore them and these people. These statements might delay your recovery because they tend to divert your thinking and focus from what you need to be working on. They unnecessarily introduce judgment and negativity into your recovery process. In this action, find a way to politely reply to those foolish and misguided statements with something like the following: *"Thank you very much for your interest. I am recovering in my own way and at my own pace. Right now, I have a plan, and I am satisfied with my progress."*

> *...find a way to politely reply to those foolish and misguided statements...*

Tailor a response that meets your needs and your style, but please keep it polite and firm. This is a good way to ensure unqualified and unskilled people stop meddling in your recovery. It is also an empowering step for you. Keep saying it and believing it. Get to work on it. Your transition to recovery is underway.

Action 7: Find the Lessons

After suffering a significant loss, in the early stages of recovery, it's normal to think that absolutely nothing good has come from the entire situation. But as you begin to deal with the loss in constructive ways, valuable lessons begin to emerge. You can think of it along these lines: If something like this ever happened to you again, then what five things would you do differently?

1. _____

2. _____

3. _____

4. _____

5. _____

In addition to what you would do differently, other important lessons surround your loss as well. Write down three of these lessons.

Example: *I learned that I need to seek input from others but make my own decisions.*

Example: *I learned that those in authority have only some of the answers.*

1. _____

2. _____

3. _____

When you write down these lessons, it shifts the power of your loss; hardship becomes a tool and a teacher. When life hands you troubles, it also provides you with valuable lessons. Most of us don't have the opportunity to choose our lessons, but the lessons are there nonetheless. These are your lessons; after all, you earned them. We might as well take advantage of them. Write down more lessons, if you can think of them. Come back to this step any time you like.

Action 8: List Positive Aspects of Your Loss

In this step, list three positive things that have come from your loss. If you think long enough and hard enough, you will find them.

Example: *I lost money, but there are positive tax consequences.*

Example: *I lost a relationship, but I gained more peace and quiet and the ability to do what I want on Saturday mornings.*

What new things have you learned? What new connections have you made? How have you strengthened your faith? You will begin to see the positive elements. I challenge you to list three positive aspects related to your loss.

1. _____
2. _____
3. _____

Action 9: Keep a Gratitude Journal

"The firm, the enduring, the simple, and the modest are near to virtue."
–Confucius

One step that truly makes a difference in your recovery is to keep a gratitude journal; it really works. Being grateful changes your brain chemistry for the better. Give thanks for the very valuable lessons that you have been given. Give thanks for all of your gifts, regardless of your loss.

Give thanks for all of your gifts, regardless of your loss.

Maybe you did not anticipate your trial. I am truly sorry that you had to go through what you went through. If there was an "undo" key, I'd surely hit it for you—but alas, life contains no undo key. Given that, you have two choices:

1. Focus on the past. Be stuck, ruminate, and recreate the past. You can choose to mourn and feel sorry for yourself. You can dedicate your future to your past.

2. Choose to put the past and your loss behind you. You can dedicate the present and the future to being open to new possibilities.

I'll assume that you picked option two. You do not know what the future holds for you. Not to worry though, be excited. Employ this helpful, future-directed question: What can you do now to make the best of your current situation? Remember to set realistic expectations for yourself and others.

You, Your Loss, and Your Recovery Are Unique

Your loss is uniquely and intensely personal. No one can share it with you. No one can take it away from you. Given that everyone's losses are unique, pursue your recovery in a manner that meets your inimitable needs.

Do not get pulled into one-size-fits-all statements and generalizations, which are generally irrelevant because:

- Each person's loss is different.

- Each person's tolerance for loss is diverse and is unique at different times.

- Each person comes from a different starting point.

- Each person possesses a varied frame of reference.

- Each person differs in his/her point of view.

- Each person holds to a different value system.

- Each person is at his/her own stage of recovery.

- Each person moves through every stage at his/her own pace.

- Each person will make progress through every stage uniquely.

- Each person will reach variable degrees of completion in each stage.

To wrap up the third E, please answer these two questions in your notebook:

- To what extent do you believe that you possess (inside of you) exactly what you need for your recovery? Why?

- To what extent do you believe that nothing is in your way and/or limits your recovery? Why?

This third E—embrace the situation—charts your individual course on your recovery journey. You can embrace your loss, not just accept it. Embrace it and own it; it is yours. Take your lessons and run with them. Express gratitude for all of your blessings; it will make you feel better and will change your perspective. Let's move on to the fourth E: envision your new future.

6. The Fourth E: Envision Your New Future

"If you think you can... or you think you can't—you're right."
– Henry Ford

Now in the fourth E, you'll begin to put your loss behind you; it will be fading fast! There are four actions in the fourth E. Given the solid foundation that you're building, it's time for you to envision a new future for yourself and your new life. Dare to dream big. You have come very far

> *...it's time for you to envision a new future for yourself and your new life.*

and have thought very differently over the past three Es. You've traveled to where you are now from the sum of your past experiences.

- You have gifts.
- You have wisdom.
- You have skills, abilities, and talents.
- You have positive attributes.
- You have your lessons.
- You have your blessings.

What is your passion? What is your dream? The keys to your recovery lie in shaping your dream. Building a business was my dream, but what is yours? Visualization is an excellent tool to tap into your passion. Now imagine that there are no boundaries. Imagine that nothing holds you back.

- There are no limits.
- There are no rules.
- There are no can'ts.

Take a few moments to clear your thoughts, get comfortable, and still your mind. Release all limitations; set them free like brightly colored butterflies in a gentle wind. You can do anything. You can be anything. Let's go.

Action 1: Envision a Future Day

> *"Only those who risk going too far can possibly find out how far they can go."*
> – T.S. Eliot

Imagine yourself five years into the future. Imagine that you are doing exactly what you want. This could be at work, at home, with your family, or with your significant other—whatever is most important to you. You are happy and filled with joy. Take in the sights, smells, and sounds around *Your resources* you. Truly engage your senses. Describe a day in *are infinite.* your future vision; go ahead and dare to dream big. Pay attention to everything around you. Your energy is boundless. Your resources are infinite. No limitations exist whatsoever. Redirect your energy to things of worth. Identify your passion. Follow your dream. Now bring those thoughts back.

- What are you doing?

- Where are you?

- Who are you with?

- How many people are around you?

- How do you feel?

- What sounds do you hear?

- What do you see? Describe the room or the setting.

- What can you smell?

- What can you touch?

- What are you wearing?

- What else is in your vision?

Take some time to fill in as many of the details of your vision as you can in your notebook. Get excited about it. Raise your energy level.

Action 2: Assess Your Vision

> *"People are like stained glass windows. They sparkle and shine*
> *when the sun is out, but when the darkness sets in;*
> *their true beauty is revealed only if there is a light from within."*
> – Elizabeth Kubler Ross

Now that you have articulated your vision, note how you feel about it. Read it over and record your reactions in your notebook. Is this the most important aspect of your life going forward? What level of energy do you feel surrounding it? How excited are you? Why? Is it like a dream come true?

Would you be amazingly happy and fulfilled doing this activity? If the answer is yes, go on to Action 3. If the answer is no, please repeat the exercise again and envision a new scene. Take your time to identify a dream that is truly important and exciting in your life. If you haven't done any envisioning work in the past, please be patient. It is a new way of thinking. Soon you'll see how empowering and energizing it is.

Action 3: Define Your Goals List

> *"I think we all have a little voice inside us that will guide us...*
> *if we shut out all the noise and clutter from our lives*
> *and listen to that voice, it will tell us the right thing to do."*
> – Christopher Reeve

Using your vision as a foundation, list your goals to turn your vision into reality. Where do you want to be? List your goals, rework them, and edit them. As you begin to refine your goals, think of them in the context of SMART goals—Specific, Measurable, Achievable, Realistic, and Time bound.

Using your vision as a foundation, list your goals to turn your vision into reality.

- Specific: Goals need to be specific so it is possible to judge whether you've attained them.

- Measurable: Goals need to be measurable, simple, and objective to see if you've reached them precisely.

- Achievable: Goals need to be reasonable and achievable. They need to be within your reach with a little stretch.

- Realistic: Goals need to be realistic given the skills, abilities, time, and resources that will be applied.

- Time bound: Goals need to have a deadline to keep you on track and to monitor your progress.

Example: *I will work overtime to earn an extra $200 in the next thirty days.*

When the list of goals starts to stabilize, select the five most important ones. List them in their order of priority by numbering them from 1-5. Review your priorities to make sure that you are comfortable with them. Now that you know what you want to do, the next step involves breaking down your goals into manageable steps.

Action 4: Break Your Goals into Manageable Steps

"An effort made for the happiness of others lifts us above ourselves."
– Lydia M. Child

Going back to your list of prioritized goals, focus on the first one. Break this goal down into discrete tasks. Do these steps take months, weeks, days, or hours? Are any of these tasks sequential? Do some tasks need to be completed before the other tasks can be started?

If a task takes longer than two weeks, split it into smaller steps. Large complex tasks are often difficult to track. A complex, multi-phased step that can only be partially checked off over an extended period can knock you off track.

If a task takes longer than two weeks, split it into smaller steps.

What support do you need? Be cognizant of tasks that depend on other tasks or other people; they need to be higher priority if they block you from moving on to the next task. Look at the overall plan. Does it make sense? Ask the following questions:

- Are these the right steps?
- Are these the only steps needed to reach the goal in its entirety?
- Will the completed goal partially or completely make your vision possible?
- Is the timeline workable to maintain momentum?
- Are the resources available in keeping with the timeline?

If the answer is no to any of these questions, rework the task list iteratively until all of the answers are yes. This is not a sprint but rather a marathon to your new future. Take the time to make the plan solid. Your plan for a new life will require all the time you need to heal.

When you've planned out the first goal, you have the option of going forward with it and executing the plan or of developing the second goal on the priority list, depending upon how important it is and how interrelated the goals are. When you are ready to execute the plan, you are ready for the fifth E—energize your world.

7. The Fifth E: Energize Your World

"All that matters is energy."
– Bruce Schneider

In the fifth E, you are ready to launch your new life. There are four actions in the fifth E. Now you possess a vision; you've built a solid foundation for your recovery and have developed a detailed action plan to make it happen. Look at how very far you have come. Your emphasis has shifted from the past, through the present, to the future.

Action 1: Execute the Plan

"Strive not to be a success, but rather to be of value."
– Albert Einstein

With the planning behind you, now it's time to act. Schedule time to do the tasks. Make a commitment to yourself to complete the required items each day or each week. Allow for contingencies and unforeseen events. Be firm, yet flexible. Push forward. If you run into a delay, rework the plan so that you are back on track. Set new target dates that are realistic from that day forward. Don't fret over missed deadlines and don't jettison the entire plan. Adjust it and keep at it. Focus your energy on your vision and your exhilaration in meeting your goal.

If you need a break, take it and then re-work the plan. Just keep moving

Just keep moving forward.
This is how winners win.

forward. This is how winners win. They don't give up; they keep at it. You are a winner, so that is what you will do too.

Action 2: Monitor the Plan

Depending upon the complexity of the tasks, you can monitor the overall action-plan progress daily or weekly.

- Is it aligned with your vision?
- What is on track?
- What is not on track?
- What needs to be changed?
- What other tasks are affected?
- What resources do you need?
- How is your energy flowing?

As you monitor your plan, you will receive new ideas about how to adjust the plan based on the current situation and any refinements in your vision. In all cases, keep your eye on the prize—think about achieving your goals and experiencing your vision. Is your dream coming into clearer focus as you allocate increasing amounts of energy toward achieving your goal? Circle back and pick up another goal when the first goal is well underway.

Action 3: Reach Out to Others

> *"Kindness is more important than wisdom, and the*
> *recognition of this is the beginning of wisdom."*
> – Theodore Isaac Rubin

In this action, extend yourself by reaching out to others, focusing out and away from yourself. Now that you have your dream in process or in place and are starting to focus your energy on that, see yourself in the context of those around you. Think of yourself as a citizen of the world.

Think of yourself as
a citizen of the world.

- Who would you like to help?

- How can you help them?

- What can you do?

- How could you get started?

- When could you start?

As a graduate in your own recovery program, you now can reach out to others in a meaningful way. Think of ways to share your story, share your gifts, focus on the future, and help everyone you can along the way. Helping others stimulates healing. High energy equals high success. High power equals high opportunity. Remove the distractions from your life and focus on your dream, your vision, and your passion. Focus and channel your energy and then go to it!

> *Remove the distractions from your life and focus on your dream, your vision, and your passion.*

Action 4: Refine Along the Way

> *"Compassion is difficult to give away because it keeps coming back."*
> – Cort Flint

The world is dynamic. Consequently, a good life plan is also dynamic.

- Is it still the right vision?

- Is it still the right goal?

- Is it still the right plan?

- Is it still the right task?

- Is it still the right deadline?

- Are the resources still the right ones?

Adjust the plan to keep a high level of energy directed toward where you want it to go. This continuous monitoring process enables you to stay on track and also be ready to take on new opportunities as they arise. Keep in mind to routinely:

- Reevaluate the situation,

- Recalibrate your activities,

- Rejuvenate the plan, and

- Reinvigorate your passion.

Go forth with energy and enthusiasm. Rock your world. To help keep up your momentum with your 5Es, I am offering my readers a free CD entitled "10 Keys to Happiness"; you only pay $1.95 for shipping. Go to http://www.BouncingBackFromLoss.com/CDbonus.

"Now is the time for all of us to become free of the fear that has kept us from joy, from creativity, from peace, from the courage to be honest. It is time to do the inspired thing, which is to live our life's purpose."
– Joseph Bailey

CHAPTER 15

Seven Common Obstacles to Recovery

"Never let yesterday use up too much of today."
– Will Rogers

When you face significant setbacks or losses in your life, it is common to try to push through these times on your own. In search of recovery—that is your only mission. A peaceful, fulfilled existence—that is the dream.

"I can make it through this," you say. But you might find that you don't have the right tools to successfully and completely overcome the loss, try as you might. The common refrain "it just takes time" rings hollow when you're the one in pain. "Easy for you to say," you might think and rightfully so.

- How can anyone possibly know how you feel?
- How could they know why you are where you are?
- Why do you feel the way you do right now?
- How will that feeling change over time?

You may find it very lonely and isolating as you search for answers to these and other important questions. You are right though; no one can feel your pain. And while you do appreciate the concern of family or friends, are they willing and able to provide you with the type of help you're looking for to overcome your loss and advance you on the road to recovery? Your goal entails simply feeling some semblance of normalcy again—to the extent that is even possible. When it seems that no one understands what you are going through, and what you've tried in the past has not worked, please rest assured that there is hope and help. Remember that you are not alone.

I identified seven potential obstacles that might block your path to recovery. These seven obstacles represent <u>key</u> blocks that might hold you back. They are common among people who have suffered significant personal loss.

Each person reacts to loss differently. You might recognize yourself in some of the obstacles, but not in others. That is to be expected. You

Each person reacts to loss differently.

might have already broken down some of the obstacles, but not others. Again, this is to be expected. Successfully breaking through blocks and overcoming these obstacles will give you the momentum and power you need to drive your own personal recovery.

Obstacle #1: Not Allowing Yourself to Grieve

Not allowing yourself to grieve for your loss robs you of the opportunity to sort through what happened; it prevents you from coming to terms with your loss. Commonly, people minimize what happened and push their feelings far below the surface, thereby never confronting or addressing the situation and their feelings about it.

Men commonly do this, but many women also react this way with an outward sign of strength. You may not see the need to grieve or suppose it's best just to push on. Especially if others depend upon you, you might believe it is more important to take care of others than to take care of yourself.

Alternatively, if others did not agree with how you acted or did not support the decisions that you made, it might be difficult for you to grieve without drawing their disapproval. This is the stiff-upper-lip camp. Ah, but being stoic in times of personal turmoil is highly overrated and can actually prolong the healing process. Any loss can be associated with a number of important and far-reaching changes in your life. In an emotional relationship, these might include loss of:

- companionship and good times,
- affection and intimacy,

- special conversations and moments,

- holidays, anniversaries, and events,

- routines and rituals,

- activity, dining, and travel partner, or

- new opportunities.

If your loss was financial, these changes might include downsized expectations, delayed gratification, or loss of:

- ability to assist your children as planned,

- ability to care for your parents,

- special activities, gifts, and vacations,

- entertainment and dining options,

- shelter and transportation options,

- plans to reduce your work hours, or

- plans to retire in the near future.

You can fill in the blanks for your specific situation. In any case, it was a significant loss to you. Your lifestyle and plans may need to change—sometimes in small ways, sometimes in big ways. So it is important to recognize the need to grieve. The grieving process enables you to start to move past the effects of your loss.

Obstacle #2: Ruminating Over the Past

Ruminating over the past focuses on looking back and reliving the details of your loss over and over and over. The movie keeps playing in your head. Every time you do not actively think about something else, the movie begins to run.

It can play first thing in the morning or as the last thing at night—over and over. It can sneak into your mind at any time. Each time the movie plays in your head, a few more facts might fall into place—another detail here, another detail there. You can trick yourself into thinking that it is actually constructive to keep going over these details. Perhaps you believe you're filling in the gaps to try to fully understand what happened—but with no end in sight.

A particularly troubling thought pattern involves questioning, "Why me?" Well, why not you? Everyone suffers with something. Honestly, they do. This just happens to be your stuff—right here and right now.

You might think that more analysis is required. But that is not what's happening. You are stuck in this movie—with no popcorn in sight. After awhile, you aren't analyzing or gaining insight. The same old movie just plays over and over. Somehow it brings a strange comfort like a long-lost friend. The movie plays in your head without you even thinking about it; wait, it's starting up again.

This type of ruminating actually causes more pain and leaves you stuck in the past without a bridge to the future. Stop the movie. The past is the past. The cost of ruminating is significant. You give up your present—and all of your life choices—by steadfastly hanging on to the past.

Obstacle #3: Recreating the Past

Recreating the past is a means of self-deception. It usually begins with a statement: "If only… I would have, or he would have, or she would have, or if this or that didn't happen." This kind of talk is a major block to your recovery.

Under this line of thinking exists an infinite number of possibilities of what might have happened or what might have turned out differently. *Everything would have been okay if only…How can the loss be undone? What might have been? If I could just change this one thing, then everything would be okay.* But it is all pure speculation and in actuality not helpful. No one can change the past, but anyone can get stuck in it.

Recreating the past only serves to avoid the real issues in facing the loss and its diverse impacts in your life going forward. This is denial, pure and simple. What happened really happened. It is what it is. So forgive and forget. The sooner you can accept it, the sooner you will be ready to move on to new and better dimensions of your life.

Obstacle #4: Avoiding the Loss with Busyness

In today's fast-paced and complex society, there is never a shortage of things to do. Hundreds of cable TV channels, millions of web pages, and a myriad of movies, games, and activities just wait to divert your attention.

After a significant loss, some advise those suffering to "keep busy." This avoidance tactic only works in the short term. Yes, you can sign up for activities five or six days a week. But sooner or later, there will be a time when you are home alone and the sadness of your loss will pervade your spirit. You can run, but you can't hide from your loss. Unless you are one of the very lucky few, just keeping busy and simply letting time pass—without doing the needed work—will likely not yield you the results and the personal recovery that you expect and deserve.

You can run, but you can't hide from your loss.

Unlike Obstacle #1 (not allowing yourself to grieve) in this obstacle (keeping yourself busy), you do see the need to grieve. These are related obstacles, but they are different. When you avoid your loss with busyness, you are not ready to formally begin the process. You keep putting it off because you are so busy. In most cases, if your loss is significant, you need to work to start to build your new life. Sooner or later, you need to do the work in order to lay a solid foundation for your recovery and future. Why settle for only a partial recovery? Why not start your healing now?

Obstacle #5: Not Acknowledging Your Role

In many situations of loss, a complex series of events took place. Things were said; decisions were made. Only you know your case and can fill in the blanks. Perhaps in your mind, the way you see it is that things were done to you. You consider yourself powerless in controlling the events that led to your loss.

Think back: You might recognize some signals or clues as to what was happening. Early warning signs almost always exist. You might not have recognized them at the time or understood their significance then, but it is likely that the signs were there in some form. It is very constructive to lay out the facts as to what you did, what assumptions you made, and what actions you took or didn't take that might have been directly or indirectly related to your loss.

- Were you listening intently?
- Were you observing closely?
- Did events begin to take on a life of their own?
- Did you relinquish control somewhere?
- Did you explain away any significant events or statements?

Only you know the answers to these questions, the particular details of your situation, and what led up to your loss. Please be open and honest when you chart out the events and assess your role in all of it. This step might open new pathways to understanding, coping, and forgiving.

Obstacle #6: Not Seeking Out the Lessons

As your recovery process begins to take root, you may face the tendency to simply put it all behind you and move on. While on the surface this sounds great, it is suboptimal. Moving on without addressing underlying issues might hamper a full recovery in the long term, especially if you do not learn the valuable life lessons. At this point, your loss cannot be reversed. Why not learn from it?

You certainly would not have chosen to bring your loss into your life, but here it is. Why not <u>decide</u> to make the best of it? And if you don't learn the lessons now, you could find yourself in the same situation repeatedly. Seeking out the lessons helps you to gain a deeper understanding of the events and of yourself. Have courage. Take a look back over the course of events.

...if you don't learn the lessons now, you could find yourself in the same situation repeatedly.

- Who did what?
- Who said what?
- What might you do differently next time?

An objective analysis of your strengths and weaknesses under pressure could be very helpful. Are you vulnerable under certain conditions but not others? These insights will provide clues into your beliefs and reactions. They will help you to assess why things worked out the way they did. Glean at least three lessons from your loss. These nuggets of wisdom can go into your life manual as you move forward.

Obstacle #7: Not Seeking Skilled Help When You Need It

By now, you might have tried several approaches to cope and deal with your loss. If you are not bouncing back and your recovery is not moving forward as you expected, plenty of sources for help are available. Each case of loss is very different and intensely personal. Please seek the level of care that best meets your individual needs based on the nature of your loss and where you are in your individual recovery process.

You are unique—truly one of a kind. Everyone enters this personal recovery process with a different background and with diverse core values. Everyone begins his/her personal recovery from a unique starting point. Everyone possesses an individualized frame of reference. As you can see, *You are unique— truly one of a kind.* personal recovery is *clearly* a case where one size does NOT fit all. Consider the many recovery options:

- You can talk with your doctor to see what medical options, if any, might meet your needs.

- Counseling with a results-based psychologist has been very effective in some cases.

- Faith-based initiatives can also be very powerful, as they were in my case.

- For extremely significant losses, talk with a grief coach specializing in your area of loss.

- Consider using the 5 Es to Recovery Coaching Program (more information can be found in the back of the book) to bounce back from your loss.

- There are literally thousands of self-help books to read if you are committed to tackling this on your own.

- Friends and family might help you by simply listening.

If help is there for you, take advantage of it—with gratitude. That help might be all that you need to be well on your way to personal recovery. Whatever path you decide to take on your personal recovery journey, make sure that it is right for you and that it meets your specific and unique needs. Decide what helps *you*.

- Are you being heard?
- Are you deciding what is best for you?
- Are you making progress?

Judge the effectiveness of the approach you take by how you feel and the progress you've made.

CHAPTER 16

Tomorrow Is a New Day

"What you love is a sign from your higher self of what you are to do."
– Sanaya Roman

1. A Brighter Future Is at Hand

"Dream no small dreams."
– Victor Hugo

No matter what has happened, no matter what your loss, today is a new day. Your best days are indeed ahead of you. Remember that I, too, was in the depths of pain with shattered dreams, suffering panic attacks, and experiencing huge financial loss. I had put off truly living for thirty-eight years in order to retire early, but the person closest to me snatched my dream away. The betrayal was absolutely devastating.

Life threw me a curve when I was one inch from the finish line. I thought it was God's will for us to be together, which was the prevailing thought in my mind as I processed the swirling emotions. I asked for guidance, but I did not receive it in a form that I could understand. But through all of the pain and anguish, ups and downs, twists and turns—I bounced back, and you can too.

> *I asked for guidance, but I did not receive it in a form that I could understand.*

Key Messages

Pain is a major catalyst for change. You did not ask for your troubles or for your pain, but here it is anyway. When you find pain and loss in your life, at least you can accept it and use it to your advantage. You can make the best of it! In dealing with your pain, the following messages are key:

- There is hope and there is help. You can bounce back.

- Be grateful for your blessings and lessons.

- Ask for forgiveness and forgive others.

- Build connections with faith, family, friends, and community.

- Find the humor in the situation, have fun, and play games.

- Imagine a new future, discover your passion, and find your joy.

You are better today than you were yesterday. You will be better tomorrow than you are today. Resilience paves the road to recovery. Focus on the big picture, your faith, and your dream. Ask yourself the following:

- How can I be more aligned with my values?

- How can I be more aligned with my vision?

- How can I be more aligned with my passion?

You are reading this book for a reason. I challenge you to absorb the messages, select the tools, implement your plan, and soar. Live your dream. Find your joy now.

2. Apply the Tools that Work for You

"Life is a process. We are a process. The universe is a process."
– Anne Wilson Schaef

We have discussed many tools including the Seven Obstacles to Recovery, the 5 Es to Recovery, and other techniques. To fully customize your recovery, select and assemble the tools that will work for you. Be resilient and transform yourself in your recovery process. By focusing on the future, the past will gradually fade into the shadows.

To fully customize your recovery, select and assemble the tools that will work for you.

Spend some time to sort through your feelings and emotions. What excites you? Find your passion. Maybe you want to start a business or work with kids. Perhaps you've dreamed of writing, working with crafts, playing music, taking a class, or ... you fill in the blank.

While you work on your feelings, take up a physically demanding activity and work out until you reach near exhaustion, if you are physically able. It benefits your body and your brain and significantly reduces the effects of stress. Intense exercise drives oxygen to your brain. Perform the exercises in intervals. Get moving—you will feel better. Also, get seven to eight hours of restful, curative sleep per day. Sleep helps to balance your hormones and, believe it or not, helps you to shed excess weight.

Look at the world around you with fresh eyes. Expect the best but strengthen yourself for the good and bad times. Develop a mindset to prevent what you can and to conquer what you can't prevent. Make the decision to start your recovery journey now. Dream big and work toward that dream with all of your heart.

> *Expect the best but strengthen yourself for the good and bad times.*

3. Your Personal Recovery Plan

"A dream becomes a goal when action is taken toward its achievement."
– Bo Bennett

"It takes as much energy to wish as it does to plan."
– Eleanor Roosevelt

As you develop your personal recovery plan, the details regarding what you want to do and when you want to do it will begin to reveal themselves. The idea is to plan for the future but live in the moment. What milestones are really important in your life? How do you currently spend your time? Does the way you spend your time help or hinder the achievement of those milestones?

> *The idea is to plan for the future but live in the moment.*

Sometimes it is difficult to get started. There are dozens of reasons why not now. But there are hundreds of reasons why. Remember to Just Say No To The Status Quo™. Doing what you did brought you to where you are, but that will not take you to where you want to be.

It is often necessary to change your attitude before you are ready to move forward. Positive thinking will accelerate your progress. Never give up. It truly does get easier. Once the wheels of your recovery start to turn, your momentum will carry you forward. Whether you chart your new course on a computer, calendar, or notebook, planning to succeed begins with defining SMART goals. I mentioned these earlier, but let's review them again.

- Specific: Goals need to be specific so it is possible to judge whether you attained them.

- Measurable: Goals need to be measurable, simple, and objective to see if you've reached them precisely.

- Achievable: Goals need to be reasonable and achievable. They need to be within your reach with a little stretch.

- Realistic: Goals need to be realistic given the skills, abilities, time, and resources that will be applied.

- Time bound: Goals need to have a deadline to keep you on track and to monitor your progress.

If you already lead a very busy life, start with one goal and carefully define the tasks that are needed to bring that goal to successful completion. Limit the number of tasks with that goal to approximately seven at a time. Define the tasks in sufficient detail and divide them so that they can each be completed within two weeks. Otherwise, it is too easy for the tasks to be lost in the daily shuffle. Segmenting your goals increases your momentum and decreases any possible feelings of being overwhelmed.

> *"Divide each difficulty into as many parts*
> *as is feasible and necessary to resolve it."*
> – Rene Descartes

As you lay out your tasks, visualize yourself crossing off a completed task. Imagine the feeling of accomplishment. Wow, you did it! You are truly on your way now. You can *Each completed task builds upon the last and grows your confidence.* experience that feeling of achievement over and over, building the momentum as you carry out your task plan. Each completed task builds upon the last and grows your confidence.

If you fall behind, don't worry. Most people do sooner or later. Life has a way of intervening in your plans and goals. Simply recalibrate the tasks with new dates and keep on going. This updated plan becomes your new plan, and suddenly you are right back on track. The process of recovery and self-development is a marathon, not a sprint. Importantly, after a setback, pick yourself up and climb back on that horse. Resilience separates the winners from the rest.

"You may have a fresh start at any moment you choose, for this thing that we call "failure" is not the falling down but the staying down."
– Mary Pickford

4. Next Steps in Your Personal Recovery

"You have to believe it's possible and believe in yourself.
Because after you've decided what you want, you have to
believe it's possible, and possible for you, not just for other people.
Then you need to seek out models, mentors, and coaches."
– Jack Canfield

This is your life. This is your now. Haven't you spent enough time going over the past? Isn't it time to imagine what your life would be like if you lived your dream?

Your future is at stake. Get excited about your future. Every day you wait, you deprive yourself and the world around you of your gifts and your joy. The next steps in your personal recovery are to decide to:

- live your life to the fullest,

- have a better future starting today,

- follow your dream,

- do whatever it takes to get there, and

- have fun along the way.

Claim your vision and find your joy now. You are in the driver's seat. Remember to enjoy the journey; plan for the future but live in the now. I wish you the best in your fabulous new future.

> *"The thing always happens that you really believe in;*
> *and the belief in a thing makes it happen."*
> – Frank Lloyd Wright

> *"Choice, not chance, determines one's destiny."*
> – Anonymous

Appendices

APPROXIMATE TIME LINE

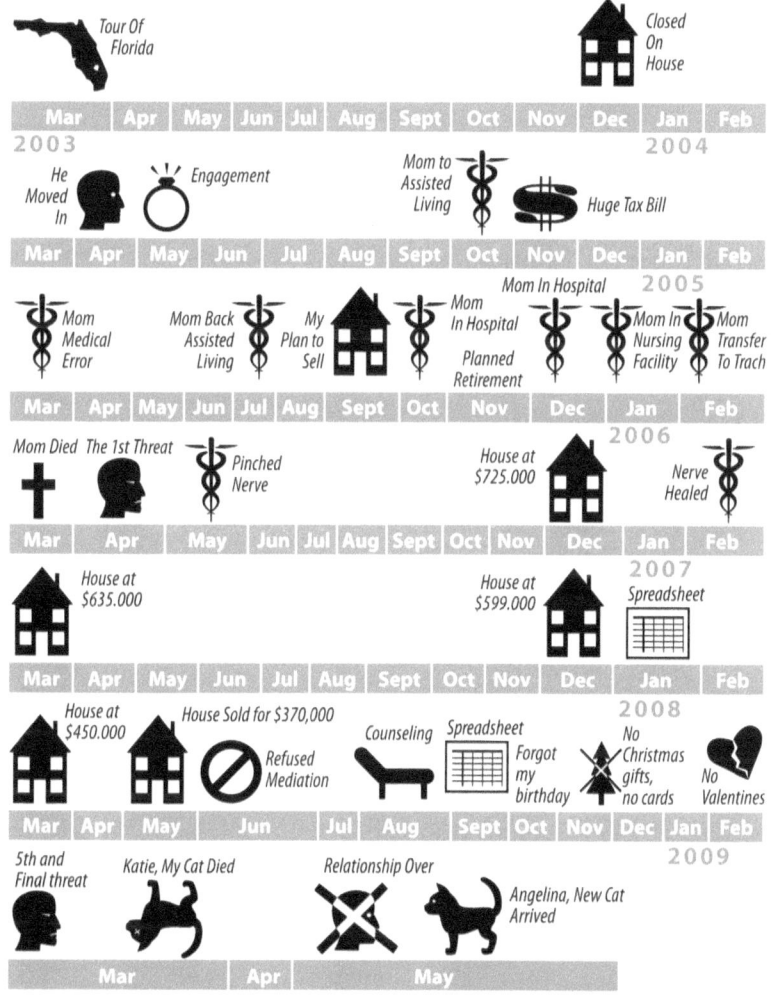

Tour Of Florida

Closed On House

| Mar | Apr | May | Jun | Jul | Aug | Sept | Oct | Nov | Dec | Jan | Feb |

2003   2004

He Moved In

Engagement

Mom to Assisted Living

Huge Tax Bill

| Mar | Apr | May | Jun | Jul | Aug | Sept | Oct | Nov | Dec | Jan | Feb |

2005

Mom Medical Error

Mom Back Assisted Living

My Plan to Sell

Mom In Hospital

Mom In Hospital

Planned Retirement

Mom In Nursing Facility

Mom Transfer To Trach

| Mar | Apr | May | Jun | Jul | Aug | Sept | Oct | Nov | Dec | Jan | Feb |

2006

Mom Died   The 1st Threat

Pinched Nerve

House at $725.000

Nerve Healed

| Mar | Apr | May | Jun | Jul | Aug | Sept | Oct | Nov | Dec | Jan | Feb |

2007

House at $635.000

House at $599.000

Spreadsheet

| Mar | Apr | May | Jun | Jul | Aug | Sept | Oct | Nov | Dec | Jan | Feb |

2008

House at $450.000

House Sold for $370,000

Refused Mediation

Counseling

Spreadsheet Forgot my birthday

No Christmas gifts, no cards

No Valentines

| Mar | Apr | May | Jun | Jul | Aug | Sept | Oct | Nov | Dec | Jan | Feb |

2009

5th and Final threat

Katie, My Cat Died

Relationship Over

Angelina, New Cat Arrived

| Mar | Apr | May |

Survey

Please take a few moments to fill out this survey and send it to BouncingBackNow@Comcast.net or go online to fill it out at: http://www. BouncingBackFromLoss.com/survey. Thank you.

1. Male or female

2. Type of loss:

Financial loss, relationship breakup, death of a parent, loss of a job, physical injury, health/disease, other _____

3. Describe your loss in two to three sentences.

_____

_____

_____

4. How did the book help you?

_____

_____

_____

5. How ready are you for recovery? _____

6. What else would you like help with?

_____

_____

_____

The 5 Es to Recovery Coaching Program™

The groundbreaking 5 Es to Recovery Program is designed to:

- Shortcut your recovery and put the past behind you—once and for all,
- Help you embrace your loss and move forward,
- Give you the support you need to get through this loss,
- Enable you to build networks for continued support, and
- Help you handle what life throws at you next.

What you get in the 5 Es to Recovery Coaching Program

- Five audio recordings focused on the 5 Es (listen on your own schedule)
- Five sixty-minute group teleclasses focused on the 5 Es with Q&A (recorded)
- Five personal one-on-one customized coaching sessions
- The 5 Es to Recovery Coaching Program™ workbook
- Five weekly tweets focused on the 5 Es
- Five weekly e-mails providing more detail on the 5 Es

- An autographed copy of *Bouncing Back: Thriving in Changing Times,* and

- Five weeks of e-mail support—based on availability.

Results that You Can Expect

At the end of the program, you will have:

- Renewed confidence to combat your loss once and for all,

- New tools to overcome your current loss and any loss in the future,

- Defined boundaries for your loss that limit it and fence it in,

- Learned the positive lessons that your loss has taught you,

- An attitude of gratitude to change your perspective of your loss,

- Realization that you have what it takes to overcome difficult problems, and

- Satisfaction and camaraderie of working with others on your personal recovery journey.

This is just what you need—and at just the right time. Remember that this groundbreaking recovery program is limited due to the one-on-one coaching. Put your personal recovery on the fast track. You deserve to have this all behind you. You can begin to experience recovery now! When you participate in the 5 Es to Recovery Coaching Program, you will have the tools and personalized support you need for your recovery.

Don't wait! Get the full details at:

http://www.bouncingbackfromloss.com

Quizzes

Controlling Relationships Quiz

1. Does your partner often correct you, interrupt you, or talk over you?

2. Does your partner answer for you when people directly ask you a question?

3. Does your partner finish your sentences before you get a chance to?

4. Does it upset your partner when you talk to others?

5. Does your partner tell you what you think or what you like?

6. When you say how you feel, does your partner disagree and tell you how you <u>really</u> feel?

7. Do you have a difficult time getting your partner to go where you want to go?

8. Does your partner opt out when you visit your family?

9. Does your partner pout or get angry when he/she doesn't get his/her way?

10. Do you have to check in frequently with your partner when you are out?

11. Does your partner pretend he/she doesn't hear your suggestions?

12. Do you give in most of the time just to keep the peace?

13. Does your partner tell you what you cannot wear (for example, no sweat pants or no jeans)?

14. Does your partner point out your "faults" for your own good?

15. Does your partner avoid taking responsibility for his/her actions?

16. Does your partner tend to forget what he/she said when it is convenient?

17. Does your partner have all the answers?

18. Does your partner treat you differently when you are with others vs. when you're alone with him/her?

19. Does your partner's behavior change under different circumstances?

20. Does your partner blame you for his/her feelings?

21. Does your partner often harshly criticize what you do and how you do it?

22. If one particular thing is not working, does your partner bring up dozens of other alleged violations?

23. Does your partner issue threats about leaving?

Interpreting Your Quiz Results:

If you answered yes to any of these questions, you could be in a controlling relationship. If you answered yes to more than eight questions, you have significant work to do to better understand the nature of your relationship, the nature of the questions and how they relate to each other, and the nature of your partner's view of you versus your view of yourself.

If you answered yes to seven or fewer of the questions, explore the particular questions in your own mind, then seek understanding and clarification as future events unfold.

As you proceed, make sure that you are not in danger or else seek the help you need before you consider approaching your partner with these questions. Review the 5 Es and the 7 Obstacles to Recovery to assist you in the healing process. There is hope, and you do have a choice!

If you answered no to all of the questions, then congratulations! You are likely in a healthy relationship where your significant other respects you.

Are You Ready For a Relationship Quiz

1. Are you sleeping regularly?
2. Are you eating healthy balanced meals?
3. Are your moods even?
4. Do you have a positive outlook on life?
5. Do you have a positive self-image?
6. Do your friends like to be around you?
7. Do you have high positive energy?
8. Do you have hobbies and outside interests?
9. Do you offer interesting conversation?
10. Do you appreciate the people around you?
11. Do you count your blessings?
12. Have you stopped talking about your last relationship?
13. Have all traces of bitterness gone?
14. Have you stopped crying about your last relationship?
15. Can you be all alone on a Saturday night without getting sad?
16. Has all of your anger subsided?
17. Are you basically happy?
18. Are you thinking about what you have to offer in a relationship vs. what you want to get out of a relationship?
19. Do you have plans for your future?
20. Are you living a full life?
21. Are you prepared to let the new person in your life stand on his/her own merits without excess baggage from the last relationship?
22. Have you forgiven your partner from your last relationship?
23. Have you moved past all of the hurts, violations, and grievances?
24. Have you fully healed your pain?
25. Do you fully realize that your prior relationship was with only one person—so that any conclusions you can draw from that relationship would only apply to that one person and no one in your future?

Interpreting Your Quiz Results:

If you answered yes to the majority of these questions, it's likely that you are ready to enter a new relationship. Congratulations on your recovery—you're doing great!

If you answered no to the majority of the questions, look over them and create a plan to continue bouncing back from your loss. Don't be discouraged. You've already come so far! With some hard work, you can choose to move forward and live your life now!

Elder Care Quiz

1. Are you in a caregivers or support program?

2. Do you know that you are doing/did everything that you could?

3. Do you know that you make/made important decisions with the best information available at the time?

4. Do you know that your loved one really appreciates everything that you are now doing or did?

5. Do you know that everything you do/did is viewed as an act of pure love?

6. Do you spend quiet time peacefully remembering the good times with your loved one?

7. Do you cherish your memories and commemorate the special things you did with your loved one on those days?

8. Do you truly celebrate your loved one's life and accomplishments?

9. Do you look at pictures and smile about the things that your loved one might have said or done at that time?

10. Do you know that your loved one wants/wanted you to be happy?

11. Do you know that by being happy you are honoring your loved one?

12. Do you know that by being happy you are in no way diminishing your devotion to your loved one?

13. Do you give thanks for the time you are/were able to spend with your loved one?

14. Do you view your time together as a precious gift?

15. Do you realize that you alone are/were able to spend that precious time with your loved one?

16. Do you openly discuss the interesting things that your loved one did?

17. Do you understand that your loved one does/did possess a generous spirit?

18. Are you living your life in a way that would make your loved one smile?

19. Do you understand and truly believe that the loss of your loved one is not the loss of their love?

Interpreting Your Quiz Results:

If you answered yes to many of these questions, it's likely that you are doing well with the difficult trial of elder care. Great job!

If you answered no to many of the questions, look them over and create a plan to continue bouncing back from your loss. You may need some more support to continue focusing on your recovery. But you can do this!

Physical Injury Quiz

1. Are you stable or getting better?

2. Are you in a rehabilitation or recovery program?

3. Have you fully researched your condition and your options?

4. Are you following the instructions to the letter?

5. Do you speak up if your condition or pain level worsens?

6. Are you the captain of your physical recovery team?

7. Have you assembled a medical dream team?

8. Do you persistently sort out conflicting opinions?

9. Can you chart your progress using objective measurements?

10. Are you maintaining a positive attitude toward your physical recovery?

11. Do you <u>know</u> that you will indeed get better?

12. Do you think long term so that you can take interim setbacks in stride?

13. Is your family supportive?

14. Do you have a support group or friends who you can talk to freely?

15. Are your close friends still actively rooting for your recovery?

16. Do you do the activities that you are able to do to minimize the impact of your injury on your life?

17. Do you conscientiously avoid anything that might set your recovery back?

18. Do you rely on your faith for spiritual support?

19. Do you help others when and where you can—even if it is only a word of encouragement?

20. Do you give thanks for your blessings?

Interpreting Your Quiz Results:

If you answered yes to many of these questions, it's likely that you are doing well with your difficult health problems. You didn't ask for those setbacks, but your progress sure is sweet!

If you answered no to many of the questions, look them over and create a plan to continue bouncing back from your loss and to construct the life that you want to live. You *can* recover!

Financial Loss Quiz

1. Are your finances stable or improving?

2. Are you on a financial remediation program?

3. Are you complying with the instructions to the letter?

4. Do you consider yourself to be <u>in charge</u> of your financial recovery?

5. Have you assembled a financial recovery dream team?

6. Have you thoroughly researched all of your options?

7. Do you persistently sort out conflicting opinions?

8. Are you actively managing any debt collection issues?

9. Have you consulted with all creditors to obtain some consideration?

10. Can you chart your financial progress using objective measurements?

11. Are you maintaining a positive attitude toward your financial recovery? Do you <u>know</u> that things will indeed get better?

12. Do you think long term so that you can take interim setbacks in stride?

13. Is your family supportive?

14. Do you have a support group or friends who you can talk to freely?

15. Are your friends still actively rooting for your financial recovery?

16. Have you openly disclosed your situation so that people do not have excessive expectations of you?

17. Have you made extra efforts to increase your revenue and income?

18. Have you taken the necessary (and perhaps drastic) steps to decrease your expenses?

19. Do you conscientiously avoid anything that might set your financial recovery back?

20. Do you carefully monitor your risk exposure?

21. Do you rely on your faith for spiritual support?

22. Do you help others in non-financial ways when and where you can—even if it is only a word of encouragement?

23. Do you give thanks for your blessings?

Interpreting Your Quiz Results:

If you answered yes to the majority of these questions, it's likely that you are doing well with the difficult trial of financial loss. Fantastic work! Life dealt you a bad hand, but you've coped and moved on!

If you answered no to many of the questions, look them over and create a plan to continue bouncing back from your loss. Review the 5 Es and the Seven Obstacles to Recovery to assist you in the healing process. Your best days are indeed ahead of you!

21 Stupid Things to Say When Someone Has Suffered a Loss

"Take no notice of the stupid things people say."
– Spanish proverb

Amateur psychologists, please be still! If you are not helping, at least don't do any more damage.

1. It is all for the best.
2. This is what was meant to be.
3. This is what you attracted; it is your fault.
4. You brought this upon yourself.
5. You should have seen it coming.
6. There had to be signs; you just weren't paying attention.
7. You must have really upset the universe to have so many things go wrong in your life.
8. Everyone else likes him. What is wrong with you?
9. You should have known what he was like from the beginning.
10. You brought him into your life, so you are responsible for everything that happened.
11. I didn't think you were a good couple anyway.
12. Everyone suffers losses, including you.
13. Other people have lost a lot more than you have.
14. Your loss is like everyone else's.

15. It's no big deal that you couldn't retire early; no one else can either.

16. You still have a job; many other people don't.

17. Did you try to talk to him about it?

18. How could you possibly wait this many years to notice his behavior?

19. Katie, your cat, died because she took on all of your grief.

20. You should have forcibly evicted him when you wanted to sell your house.

21. I know people who have gotten over a long relationship in two months; what is taking you so long?

Suggested Reading List

Bandler, Richard. *Get the Life You Want: The Secrets to Quick and Lasting Life Change with Neuro-Linguistic Programming*, (Deerfield Beach, FL: Health Communications Inc., 2008).

Chopra, MD, Deepak. *Quantum Healing – Exploring the Frontiers of Mind/Body Medicine*, (New York: Bantum New Age, 1989)

Dyer, Wayne W. *Change Your Thoughts - Change Your Life: Living the Wisdom of the Tao*, (Carlsbad, California: Hay House, 2007)

Engel, Beverly. *Healing Your Emotional Self*, (Hoboken, NJ: Wiley, 2006)

Evans, Patricia. *Controlling People – How to Recognize, Understand, and Deal with People Who Try to Control You,* (Avon, MA:Adams Media, 2002)

Goleman, Daniel. *Emotional Intelligence – Why it Can Matter More Than IQ,* (New York: Bantam Books, 1997)

Harris, Bill. *Thresholds of the Mind: Your Personal Road Map to Success, Happiness, and Contentment* (Beaverton, OR, Centerpointe Press, 2007).

Helmstetter, Shad. *The Self-Talk Solution*, (New York: William Morrow, 1987)

Hicks, Esther and Jerry. *The Astonishing Power of Emotions – Let Your Feelings Be Your Guide*, (Carlsbad, California: Hay House, 2007)

Kabat-Zinn, Jon. *Arriving at Your Own Door – 108 Lessons in Mindfulness*, (New York:Hyperion, 2007)

Katie, Byron. *Loving What Is – Four Questions that Can Change Your Life*, (New York: Harmony Books, 2002)

Myers, David G. *The Pursuit of Happiness – Discovering the Pathway to Fulfillment, Well-Being, and Enduring Personal Joy,* (New York: HarperCollins, 2002)

Orloff, MD, Judith. *Emotional Freedom – Liberate Yourself from Negative Emotions and Transform Your Life*, (New York: Harmony Books, 2009)

Paul, Margaret. *Inner Bonding: Becoming a Loving Adult to Your Inner Child*, (San Francisco:HarperCollins, 1992)

Schneider, Bruce D. *Energy Leadership- Transforming Your Workplace and Your Life from the Core,* (Hoboken, NJ: Wiley, 2008)

Seligman, Martin E. *Learned Optimism – How to Change Your Mind and Your Life*, (New York, Random House, 2006)

Shimoff, Marci. *Happy for No Reason – Seven Steps to Being Happy From the Inside Out*, (New York: Free Press, 2008)

Singer, Blair. *Little Voice Mastery: How to Win the War Between You Ears in 30 Seconds or Less and Have an Extraordinary Life,* (Xcel Press, 2008).

Steadman, Lisa. *It's a Breakup Not a Breakdown*, (Avon, MA: Polka Dot Press, 2007)

Stoop, David. Y*ou Are What You Think*, (Grand Rapids: Revell, 2006)

Tolle, Eckhard. *A New Earth – Awakening to Your Life's Purpose,* (New York: Plume, 2006)

Vernick, Leslie. *The Emotionally Destructive Relationship: Seeing It, Stopping It, Surviving It* (Eugene, OR, Harvest House, 2007).

Winter, Aurora. *From Heartbreak to Happiness, An Intimate Diary of Healing*, (Sedona, AZ:Sam Page LLC, 2005)

About the Author

Donna Marie Thompson, PhD, is a successful businesswoman who has come out on top of more than her share of reverses and adversity. Based on what she learned from successfully dealing with challenges head-on, she developed a system of recovering from loss. She has become a popular speaker and writer on the topic, and has developed a thriving practice as an empowerment coach.

Donna Marie is a featured author in the best-selling book *Bouncing Back: Thriving in Changing Times.* She has written numerous articles and inspirational blog posts and created a variety of self-help audios and videos to assist people through difficult times. Donna Marie lives near Washington, DC where she works, writes, and hosts the "Bouncing Back Now" program on Blog Talk Radio.

BUY A SHARE OF THE FUTURE IN YOUR COMMUNITY

These certificates make great holiday, graduation and birthday gifts that can be personalized with the recipient's name. The cost of one S.H.A.R.E. or one square foot is $54.17. The personalized certificate is suitable for framing and will state the number of shares purchased and the amount of each share, as well as the recipient's name. The home that you participate in "building" will last for many years and will continue to grow in value.

Here is a sample SHARE certificate:

YES, I WOULD LIKE TO HELP!

I support the work that Habitat for Humanity does and I want to be part of the excitement! As a donor, I will receive periodic updates on your construction activities but, more importantly, I know my gift will help a family in our community realize the dream of homeownership. **I would like to SHARE in your efforts against substandard housing in my community!** *(Please print below)*

PLEASE SEND ME _____ SHARES at $54.17 EACH = $ $_____

In Honor Of: _____

Occasion: (Circle One)   *HOLIDAY*   *BIRTHDAY*   *ANNIVERSARY*

      OTHER: _____

Address of Recipient: _____

Gift From: _____ *Donor Address:* _____

Donor Email: _____

I AM ENCLOSING A CHECK FOR $ $_____ PAYABLE TO HABITAT FOR HUMANITY <u>OR</u> PLEASE CHARGE MY VISA OR MASTERCARD *(CIRCLE ONE)*

Card Number _____ Expiration Date: _____

Name as it appears on Credit Card _____ Charge Amount $ _____

Signature _____

Billing Address _____

Telephone # Day _____ Eve _____

PLEASE NOTE: Your contribution is tax-deductible to the fullest extent allowed by law.
Habitat for Humanity • P.O. Box 1443 • Newport News, VA 23601 • 757-596-5553
www.HelpHabitatforHumanity.org

www.ingramcontent.com/pod-product-compliance
Lightning Source LLC
Chambersburg PA
CBHW030432290526
45786CB00001B/252